# TYPICAL PIP!

Daydreams and Wanderings in England, France, and Spain, and the Astonishing Kindness of People Along the Way

Pippa Hoffman

For information: typicalpip@gmail.com

Production and creative:
jonathangullery.design@gmail.com

FIRST EDITION

ISBN Print: 979-8-9897166-0-9
ISBN Ebook: 979-8-9897166-1-6

Printed in the United States of America

# Contents

*To Dale, Kent, James, Elana,*
*Alek, Sawyer and Mila*

# Introduction

began this memoir in April 2020 at home in New York as Covid 19 surged. It was a scary time for all, uncharted territory. There were upsides, however: working from home rather than driving an hour north to my office; long walks in the countryside with my husband, Dale; video chats with family and friends in Europe and the U.S. Everyone was in the same situation—there was no escaping this pesky virus.

In addition to writing and daydreaming—a lifelong pastime—I began painting scenes from previous travels: rocky coves I had photographed in Bermuda and, closer to home, scenes of Hudson River sunsets. I played my guitar, wrote in my journal, and started to feel infused with a sense of possibility despite the obvious limitations imposed by the pandemic.

The following are recollections of my early life in England and Europe until my journey took me to the United States. Part One, "England," covers my childhood in the Sussex countryside. Part Two, "France and Spain," is about traveling in Europe from age seventeen to twenty-four. As the tale unfolded, I realized it was primarily a tribute to the astonishing kindness of those I met along the way. There were scary situations and narrow escapes, but my overall experience was overwhelmingly positive.

Another realization was that I was, somehow, re-discovering my essence—the core of who I am despite the inevitable passing of years.

An optimist by nature, I tend to live in the moment, but it was helpful to reexamine and maybe rekindle those innate, quirky elements that may have been buried over time. Refusing to take myself too seriously, I offer these pages in a light-hearted yet what I hope is an authentic way.

The crafting of my story is imperfect, but I've given it my best shot. I've tried to be as faithful to memory as possible, and I apologize to those I skimmed over or left out entirely and for any inadvertent errors. I'm grateful to friends who permitted me to use their names and to tell our shared stories, and I changed the names and some details of those with whom I've lost touch.

Lastly, having lived in the United States for over half my life, I used American English spelling. However, my childhood vocabulary is firmly rooted in the British Isles and Europe, and words that may be unfamiliar to American readers are "translated" in parenthesis.

This is dedicated to friends and family on both sides of the Atlantic.

We all have a story to tell—what's yours?

New York, January 2024

# ENGLAND

# CHAPTER 1

# Beginnings

My parents, Bill Chamberlain and Joyce Goddard, both Londoners, met and married during the Second World War. Dad was a radio communications officer in the Merchant Navy, while Mum worked in sales for Singer Sewing Machines.

After their first date on Richmond Common, Mum suggested they get together the following Tuesday, but Dad, knowing he would be at sea by then, surprised her—and maybe himself—with a marriage proposal. His imminent departure meant a hurried ceremony by special license, leaving no opportunity for photos of their brief courtship or wedding.

"The ship came around to Southampton, and we had two days together," Mum recalled. "Then it left, and I didn't see any more of him for a year and a half. I went back to work, and that was that. In those days, you didn't know if you'd see your sweetheart again—you could never be certain."

During the London Blitz, Mum was accustomed to hearing German V-1 flying bombs, known as doodlebugs, overhead.

"The most frightening part was the silence when the engine cut out because that meant the bomb was coming down. If one landed on you, you'd had it!"

Mum was matter-of-fact in describing the terror of the London Blitz, but I detected sadness in her eyes and knew she lost several good friends in the war. I now understand that it didn't feel long ago to her, even though it seemed to me in the vague, distant past.

Dad made it through the war despite sustained U-boat attacks on Merchant Navy vessels, especially when delivering supplies from Canada to Murmansk in Northwestern Russia. He was tasked with receiving and dispatching Morse code communications, a job with the Navy nickname "Sparks." As a child, oblivious to the dangers Dad had faced, I enjoyed playing with his Morse code tapper and learning rudimentary signals, such as SOS.

After the war, having been discharged from the Navy, Dad continued to work with sensitive radio transmissions on land with the Diplomatic Wireless Service. In the early 1950s, he was transferred to Singapore for two and a half years, where he and my mother lived with the ex-pat community. They socialized at the polo club and were allocated a housekeeper and driver—a different reality from their humble beginnings in London. Mum said they "had a whale of a time!" The first photo I saw of my parents together was taken in Singapore: Mum with thick, wavy brown hair, wearing a floral midi dress; Dad dressed in tropical whites—both slim and smiling for the camera. Another photo of that time shows them seated around a dinner table with ex-pats and a smattering of locals. Dad is wearing a silly hat, drinks are flowing, and everyone seems to be enjoying themselves.

Back in England, Mum became pregnant for the first time at 39. Dad was 42. I was born in Northampton, in the English Midlands, where we remained for a year. My birth certificate says Philippa Rae Chamberlain, but I'm generally called Pip, Pippa, or Pippi—I answer to all of them. A late surprise to my parents; I'm an only child.

*Mum and Dad in Singapore*

There are scant stories surrounding my birth—Mum was "drugged up to the eyeballs," as she expressed it, and Dad wasn't present, as was customary in those days. The only information Mum volunteered was a vague memory:

"You had something on your head when you were born." Mum didn't always make sense—one of her most endearing qualities.

Around my first birthday, Dad was transferred to southeast England, and we settled in the village of Crowborough, where my parents spent the rest of their lives.

# CHAPTER 2

# Apples and Tadpoles

Crowborough lies high on a beacon in the Sussex countryside and borders the Ashdown Forest, an expanse of bracken-covered hills dotted with pine trees, yellow gorse bushes, and meandering streams. This is Winnie the Pooh country, as A.A. Milne wrote his tales of Christopher Robin, Pooh Bear, and friends from his home on the forest.

My parents rented a flat in Craigmore Hall, a four-story, red-brick Victorian with a view over a terraced back garden surrounded by oak, beech, and chestnut trees. I made secret camps in the garden's thick foliage, and my favorite spot was where my father set up a swing under the branches of a tree. Aside from the dreamy hours spent swinging there, I enjoyed climbing to the tree's top—a perfect lookout.

Beyond the garden's perimeter, a steep path wound down through an abandoned orchard, its trees surrounded by brambles and nettles. I helped my parents gather apples in the autumn, getting stung by nettles and rubbing the sore areas with dock leaves that grew conveniently nearby. I recall apples scattered around my bedroom floor, and "apple" was my first word.

Continuing down the orchard path, a narrow stream led to a small pond from which, each spring, I collected frog spawn in a bucket, watching the dots within the glutenous mass transform into tadpoles before returning them to the pond. A curious child, I often continued along the stream's path, squeezing under a fence and into a meadow where horses grazed. I've always been fascinated by what lies around a corner or over a hill.

Although often alone, I don't remember feeling particularly lonely as a child, although I was excited at four years old when a family moved into one of the flats, and I had friends to play with in the garden.

*On my swing*

Entering Craigmore Hall, we passed through an expansive, echoing hallway, from which rose a wide Victorian staircase with carved wooden banisters—perfect for sliding down. Each floor housed a pair of two-bedroom flats, and ours was on the third floor.

From the main hallway, stone steps led down to a damp-smelling basement containing several creepy, cobweb-filled rooms. Once a wine cellar, the basement had long since been abandoned, and I found it thrilling, if a little scary. By contrast, at the top of the house was a large, airy attic, originally a billiard room, bordered with high, rectangular stained-glass windows. I delighted in taking friends down to the spooky basement and up to the cheerier attic, staging dramatic games and looking for secret passages.

*Craigmore Hall*

I think Mum felt constricted in our flat—dragging groceries and a small child up three flights of stairs. This wasn't Singapore. We didn't own a car, refrigerator, telephone, or washer-dryer. Our black and white television was invariably "on the blink," with the picture scrolling and fading or disappearing altogether. The "sound radio," as Mum called it, was her primary source of entertainment, with its afternoon plays and musical offerings, and we both sang along to popular songs during a regular Saturday morning children's program.

One game I recall was when we each sang a line from an aria based on the eighteenth-century opera *Orpheus and Eurydice*:

"Eurydice! Eurydice!" sang Mum, waiting for my response.

"Ah, hear me," I sang back (although I couldn't pronounce my h's back then, so it sounded more like "Ah, 'ere me." Then Mum would repeat.

"Eurydice! Eurydice!"

And I would withhold my response, giggling, at which Mum would exclaim, "Oh no, she's gone out! Where did she go?" to more giggling.

The soundtrack of my childhood was Mum singing—while cooking, hanging out the washing, or boiling kettles of water for her endless cups of tea. Her repertoire and range were remarkable, and she was sometimes invited to perform at her Women's Institute. Mum's songs still pop into my consciousness to this day.

Mum was a romantic who enjoyed classic Hollywood films, music, literature, and poetry – particularly the tragic poets of the First World War. She also loved the idea of Paris, with its artistic, literary, and bohemian connections. A lifelong student of the French language, she could often be heard singing "La Vie En Rose," "Je Ne Regrette Rien," and other Edith Piaf songs.

Being of a somewhat sensitive disposition, Mum retreated to the broom cupboard, away from any windows, whenever she heard thunder, refusing to emerge until the storm had passed. Not sharing this phobia, I was dispatched to the living room at intervals to check on the weather and, when old enough, brought her cups of tea during protracted thunderstorms.

Dad was more subdued. He enjoyed bird-watching, studying Spanish, tackling math problems, and drinking a pint of beer (or several) at the local pub. Walking to the pub, dressed in his navy-blue duffle coat, with binoculars hanging from his neck, he was constantly on the lookout for birds. On noticing an unusual species, he would say "Hello," stabilize himself with the wide stance of a former sailor, bring the binoculars to his eyes, and then reach for a pencil to enter the sighting in his notebook. His nickname in the village was "the hooded crow."

Mum wasn't thrilled that Dad frequented the pub daily, participating in the tradition of each of his group of cronies buying a round of drinks. One of her favorite comments was, "He has two hobbies, and they're both beer!" at which Dad would look sheepish and smile. As a long-term sailor with a naturally shy disposition, Dad's access to social acceptance was firmly grounded in pub life. He was morally decent and kind, unfailingly devoted to Mum, but not in a romantic or demonstrative fashion from my perspective. There was some disappointment on her part, but I believe they both did their best.

Neither of my parents ever learned to drive—my dad, due to vision problems, for which he eventually underwent cataract surgery. Mum tried to learn but never quite got the hang of it. I recall sitting in the rear seat during her driving lessons, conducted in the car of a rather grumpy neighbor. He got upset when I passed the time by drawing stick figures in the window's condensation. Perhaps he wasn't the best driving instructor for Mum, either, because she eventually gave up trying to learn.

Mum walked the two-thirds of a mile to Crowborough village almost daily, with me in tow. We stopped at the greengrocer's, the butcher's, the library, and the bakery, waiting our turn in each. The bakery was my favorite because I was allowed to pull off and eat a chunk of warm crust from the end of the loaf. Skinny and energetic with a mop of auburn hair, I always found it hard to wait between meals.

I recall the thrill of Dad taking me to see *Planet of the Apes* and *Zulu* at a cinema in the village, with the added delight of a "Choc ice" ice cream bar during intermission. The cinema was later replaced by Crowborough's first supermarket, simplifying the shopping process.

Dad continued to work for the Diplomatic Wireless Service at a remote location on the Ashdown Forest. He never talked about work, and Mum said it was "very hush-hush." I'm not sure even she knew what his job entailed. Dad rode his bicycle four miles there and back each day through gale-force winds, driving rain, and the occasional snowstorm.

When I was about eight, my parents bought me a second-hand, red Raleigh bicycle, and bikes became my primary local transportation until I was sixteen, allowing me to accompany Dad on rides through the countryside, stopping at local pubs for refreshments.

*Trying out my new bike with Mum*

I'm grateful to my parents for giving me their love of travel and a positive outlook on life. From my mother, I inherited a passion for all things European, some musical ability, and a sense of fun. From my father, I gained practical aspects, which may not have kicked in until I was older but have proven invaluable over time. Plus, I don't get seasick!

# CHAPTER 3

# Naughty Little Philippa

Mum and I counted down the days to kindergarten with excitement and some trepidation on my part. Hookstead School for Girls was in a red-brick Victorian with a formal rose garden in front and a vegetable garden leading to tennis courts in the rear. I was not happy. Students ranged from ages four to eighteen, and I was scared of the "big girls," who looked like grown-ups but wore the same school uniform as the four-year-olds, which was confusing. One day, a hide-and-seek game was arranged, where younger girls were supposed to find the older ones. I wandered past the vegetable garden and saw two big girls half-concealed in a bamboo thicket. The girls giggled, I froze—and then hurried away.

I tried to get out of school. I said my leg hurt, motioning vaguely to my left calf, but it didn't work. Over time, I made some friends and got used to the idea that I'd probably be there until I was a big girl myself.

My kindergarten teacher was dedicated, and I'm sure she was wonderful overall, but she scared me. One day, emerging from a daydream, I noticed her steaming down the aisle between desks, obviously furious. I recall thinking someone was in trouble, and that someone turned out to be me.

"Naughty little Philippa," she exclaimed, slapping me on the leg and pausing to glare at me before returning to her desk. What had I done? I had no idea. I looked around at my classmates for clues but didn't dare say anything. I still don't know. My report cards said I was bright but that my head was "in the clouds."

At home, Mum was my anchor and my main companion. Dad worked rotating eight-hour shifts, including weekends, and was often at work or sleeping. When Mum was around, I felt safe. Whenever I arrived home, and there was no one there, I waited anxiously at the window overlooking the driveway, my stomach churning, until she appeared around the corner and I could relax.

My secondary companion was my bear, Big Ted. A cut above the average teddy bear, despite the name, Ted was intelligent looking, with handsome features and light blond fur. Today, over sixty years later, he is perched on my bookcase, watching me type, a little worse for wear yet still dignified.

A clue to Mum's personality lies in the names she gave my rag dolls: one was Eartha (after singer/actress Eartha Kitt), and another Ethel (after singer Ethel Merman). My favorite game involved my dolls, Big Ted and I being tossed in a storm at sea—my bed serving as the boat. As, one by one, the dolls fell overboard onto the floor, I jumped heroically into the swirling waves to rescue them, throwing each back onto the boat and safety. Wondering where this idea came from, I now remember that Dad often read Greek mythology to me at bedtime—stories of Perseus and Jason and the Argonauts. Thrilling, as well as the source of many nightmares, these adventure stories may have given me the notion that the hero's journey was something that I, too, might undertake one day.

When I was old enough to read, my favorite books were adventure series such as *The Famous Five* and *The Secret Seven* by Enid Blyton. I don't recollect ever dreaming about being a fairy princess or of a future Prince Charming rescuing me on his white horse. My one takeaway from fairy tales—*Snow White*, to be exact—was to steer clear of red apples at all costs. Who would want to be poisoned by fruit?

Mum didn't work and relished being a "housewife"—a step up from her working-class roots—enjoying her free time. I accompanied her wherever she went, often visiting her friends for tea with animated conversation and jokes that went over my head. Fortunately, Mum's friends could be counted on to provide chocolate biscuits and orange squash, a soft drink we didn't have at home, which helped relieve the boredom.

I also tagged along to Mum's art classes at the local community center, where I remember painting alongside her and being proud of my rendition of a house—until the instructor stopped by and, in a loud voice, pronounced it "fire engine red," and I was crushed. Mum continued with art classes for many years, venturing onto the Ashdown Forest in summer, equipped with paints and brushes, a flask of tea, and a sausage roll for sustenance despite the frequent rain showers and ensuing mud. I still have some of her paintings to this day.

Mum tried her best to find activities for me, her shy and somewhat awkward child. First was ballet, but at six years old, I couldn't tell my left from my right without holding a pencil, and they didn't provide pencils in ballet class. Perhaps being left-handed added to this confusion, but I felt humiliated and gave up after a few lessons. Looking back, dancing would have been fun if the teacher had been more understanding. I certainly enjoyed disco dancing later.

We had a piano at home, and I attempted to learn the "Early Melodies" tutorial. At some point, it became apparent that I was memorizing the material rather than reading the music, and I stopped playing. Mum, however, continued, graduating from "Early Melodies" to "Fur Elise,"

"Moonlight Sonata," and other classical pieces. She gave it her all, punctuating the music with a colorful "bugger and blast it" when hitting a wrong note.

Next was Brownies, where I was in the elf patrol. A somewhat scruffy elf, I wore a crumpled brown uniform dress with a yellow neck scarf. The troop met in a church hall, where we played games, sang songs, and were constantly reminded to "be prepared" and to be neat and tidy. I wasn't excited about Brownies but continued into Girl Guides, where we participated in Crowborough's annual Carnival and Bonfire Night. Riding on a flatbed lorry one year, my troop joined the parade in our school uniforms, waving hockey sticks at onlookers and imitating the unruly boarding school students from the popular film series *St. Trinian's*. An excellent chance to let off steam!

Crowborough Carnival was a highlight of our town's year. A few days before the festivities, an empty field close to our home was transformed into a colorful fairground with rides, games, and food stands. My favorite ride was the switchback, a massive roundabout with an undulating floor holding an array of brightly colored animals, cars, and motorbikes. The ride was exciting during the week, but on Friday and Saturday nights, my friends and I held tight as the lights went out, a siren sounded, and the ride went extra fast for a few delightful seconds. We also rode chair-o-planes, "dodgem" bumper cars, and a rocket-shaped "dive-bomber" —all accompanied by a sound system blasting out Tom Jones singing "Delilah" along with other hits of the era.

In addition to the fair, on bonfire night itself, the afore-mentioned parade of creative floats, marching bands, and local organizations made its way around the streets of Crowborough, ending up on the village green where fireworks erupted, and a huge bonfire burned in the dark. Part of the excitement was having free rein to roam the fair and village with friends on carnival night. I've seen many parades over the years, but none compares with the creativity and delight of Crowborough's Carnival when I was young.

# CHAPTER 4

# Sundays at Home and a First Trip to Europe

Sunday mornings were reserved for church with Dad during my early years. We walked to the village green, with its Roman Catholic church on one side and the larger All Saints Anglican, which we attended, on the other. Dad and I raced each other across the green each week until I got too fast for him. We dutifully sat through the service and, on the way back, stopped off at the White Hart pub, where he went in for a pint of beer while I waited outside with a packet of crisps and pineapple juice (children were not permitted into pubs until age 14). I spent many hours outside various pubs with similar refreshments in my youth. Nowadays, bouncy castles and petting zoos entertain children in rear gardens, but back then, it was just me and my dreamy thoughts.

Back home, Mum had prepared a Sunday lunch of roast lamb, roast potatoes, and Brussels sprouts with Yorkshire pudding. Mum restricted her church attendance to Christmas and Easter when she sang at the top of her voice. I loved Mum's singing at home, but it was acutely embarrassing in church, so I was okay with her staying home most Sundays.

We ate at a small mahogany table in the bay window of our living room. Our tablecloth was decorated with colorful portraits of the unfortunate souls beheaded by King Henry VIII: Thomas Cromwell, Anne Boleyn, and Sir Thomas More, among others. I particularly remember Henry's doomed fifth wife, Catherine Howard, gazing up at me as I awaited my pudding. I never asked how this macabre piece of linen became part of our lives—maybe a souvenir from a relative's visit to the Tower of London.

At home, I enjoyed playing church. With the sofa back serving as my pulpit, I presided over my parents and any visiting relatives in a service that involved hymns, prayers—for which they frustratingly refused to kneel—and a sermon. If I got stuck or bored mid-sermon, I would end with a dramatic, "And Jesus got up and flew out the window," gesticulating to the window of our flat for emphasis.

Hookstead School closed when I was eight, so my good friend Debbie and I transferred to St. John's Primary School. St. John's was attached to a small church where the whole school attended services every Wednesday morning. The service seemed more Catholic than Protestant, with the Greek *Kyrie eleison* included in the service and brass incense burners swung on chains.

Another memory of St. Johns was during 1966, the 900th anniversary of the famous 1066 Battle of Hastings, when the school staged a reenactment of the battle on its sloping playing field. It was a big deal, and I chose to be a Norman invader, wearing a homemade cardboard helmet with a flimsy protective nosepiece. We stormed the Saxon stronghold, where history tells us King Harold was killed by an arrow to the eye, resulting in our being ruled by the French—according to my understanding at the time. This was the last time Britain was successfully invaded, and the victory was immortalized in the famous Bayeux Tapestry, created a few years after the battle and housed, understandably, in France.

St. John's also provided my first European trip—a delightful three-day visit to Belgium and Holland via ferry. This was my first time away from my parents for a few days, and the whole experience felt wonderfully foreign. I recall purchasing a tiny lace placemat for Mum in Bruges and Debbie getting bitten by a dog, for which she needed a tetanus shot.

A cruise to Norway was offered by St. Johns the following year, but I didn't mention it to my parents, as I assumed it was expensive and that we didn't have the money.

# CHAPTER 5

# Mudlarks in Portsmouth

Each summer, Mum, Dad, and I boarded a steam train from Crowborough for a two-week visit to Dad's mother in Worthing on the Sussex Coast. Grandma's life had not been easy, as my grandfather, Francis Chamberlain, died on his way back from the battle of Gallipoli during World War One. Unable to earn a living and care for her three small boys, Grandma enrolled them in an orphanage school. Dad told me he was bullied in the orphanage. He tried collecting postage stamps there, but the other boys stole them, even when he hid them under his pillow. Not the happiest of childhoods.

I think it fair to say Grandma was not the cuddly type—probably due to the practical challenges life had dealt her. She was a chain smoker, and I was fascinated by the column of ash that collected on the tip of her cigarette—seemingly up to an inch—without falling off. Grandma kindly provided meals during our stay and occasionally accompanied us to a local beach but, more often, stayed at home. She kept a box of small toys that I enjoyed inspecting each year, and I have vague memories of playing with my young cousins, Richard, Rupert, and Robin, who lived nearby. My parents and I walked to the beach in Worthing each day, strolling along the promenade and playing mini-golf at a seafront course. We paddled in the sea, swimming when it wasn't too cold, negotiating ever-present mounds of seaweed to reach the water.

*With Dad on the beach in Worthing*

One highlight of our stay was an annual day trip from Worthing to Portsmouth, forty miles down the coast. In Portsmouth harbor, we climbed aboard Admiral Lord Nelson's ancient ship, HMS Victory, in dry dock. I recall being fascinated by the cannons, the cramped sleeping quarters on board, and the exact place on deck where Nelson died during the battle of Trafalgar in 1805.

Later that day, we took a ferry to the nearby Isle of Wight. One bewildering element was when, before boarding the ferry, we crossed a high bridge under which children, covered in gooey black mud, begged for coins. I was confused and alarmed—did these children have parents and homes to go to? Why were they diving into the mud, far below, reappearing with coins tossed from the bridge by passers-by? Years later, I learned about the mudlarks—children who scavenged for coins in Portsmouth harbor during the nineteenth and twentieth centuries, for whom a statue has now been erected there. And yes, they had families, their mothers sometimes watching their antics from nearby. Mudlarking was, apparently, a source of pocket money for sweets or trips to the cinema for local children of limited means.

As a former sailor, Dad instructed me to have "one hand for the ship and one hand for yourself" when negotiating the stairs during the brief ferry trip. On reaching the Isle of Wight, we toured its picturesque villages by bus, stopping to walk along a cliff path to the Needles rock formation at the western point. I remember watching rain lashing against the bus window one day. The water seeped through the upper window, trickling down, and looked so fresh and inviting that I put out my tongue to sample it. Of course, it tasted disgusting, and I felt sick on the return train ride to Grandma's.

# CHAPTER 6

# Brighton Rock

My other grandma, Gladys Goddard, whom we called Nan, lived in the seaside resort of Brighton, also home to Mum's sister, Elsie. Mum and I took the double-decker bus there several times a year, watching sheep grazing in the Sussex countryside from the front seat of the upper deck as we drove along narrow country roads.

Auntie Elsie's flat was on a subsidized housing estate, and I loved visiting—first with Mum and, in later years, by myself. Elsie was clever and kind, with a good sense of humor and a no-nonsense wisdom that differentiated her from my mum, who tended to be more of a dreamer. Elsie called me Pippi and never talked down to me like some adults. She had a Cairn Terrier named Katie and two lively budgerigars who could say a few words. Not having any pets at home, I enjoyed playing with the dog, watching her scoot around the flat chasing a ball, her toenails clattering on the linoleum floor as she ran.

Elsie's two children, Christine and Paul, were 15 and 12 years older than me. Paul joined the Navy at 16, so he wasn't around much then, but Christine and I walked Katie in a local park and played in a nearby recreation ground. Christine also introduced me to a chocolate bar with little holes called an Aero. The Beatles' song, "The Long and Winding Road," popular then, reminds me of the happy times we spent together. Sadly, Christine passed away from Covid when I started writing this memoir.

*Christine with her son, Gareth*

After visiting Auntie Elsie, Mum and I continued by bus to visit her mum, Nan, in her studio flat close to the sea. The studio was full of exotic ferns, my height or taller, giving it a jungle-like feeling. While Nan brewed our tea, I wandered over to her easel with its current canvas, paintbrushes, and half-squeezed tubes of oil paint. Nan meticulously copied works of the great masters, and I recall renditions of mythological nymphs and fawns. I loved those paintings and still have her miniature version of *The Source* by Jean Auguste Dominique Ingres, a neo-classical depiction of a nude woman standing by a waterfall.

Nan also created many of her clothes, knitting jackets and dresses in intricate patterns and pairing them with ornate pins and fancy hats. Nan had been poor for much of her life, but, meeting her, you would think the opposite, as she was well-spoken and well-read. She also loved to sing and patiently taught me to harmonize to "Come into the Garden, Maud" and "Sweet and Low," songs based on Alfred Lord Tennyson's poetry from the nineteenth century. Nan read tea leaves and had a crystal ball, but I wasn't aware of that then. I'm unsure if she was serious or did it "for a lark." I know she was a delightful and loving grandmother with a sense of humor that may have come from her Cockney, East London roots.

*Dancing with Nan*

While in Brighton, Mum and I walked along the promenade, indulging in fish and chips, candy floss, and Brighton Rock (large peppermint sticks with a pink sugar coating). We walked out onto the famous West Pier, sometimes in driving rain, dodging into an arcade to try our luck on the penny slots and other games with their flashing lights and exotic names. I think Mum enjoyed those games even more than I did, and I recall her often saying, "Come on. Let's have another go!" when we played together. One advantage of having a mother who seemed like a child at heart was that she never tired of having fun.

One summer, when home from the Navy, my cousin Paul took me out on his tiny sailboat alongside Brighton Pier. Getting past the initial waves was challenging—this was a boat you sat on, not in—but I trusted Paul and always enjoyed his company when he was around.

*Paul and Pauline's wedding day*

Brighton was also where Paul and his fiancée Pauline were married at a beautiful old church when I was eleven. Paul's sister, Christine, was the maid of honor, and I was a bridesmaid. We wore satiny, lime-green dresses with lacey bodices and had a lovely time celebrating the newlyweds with our entire family, including Nan, who was immaculately dressed for the occasion.

Paul and Pauline set up their home high on the South Downs, not far from Brighton, and are still there as I write. I have always enjoyed visiting them and their family and walking on the nearby wind-swept hills. As an only child, I value Paul as my almost sibling—my down-to-earth, sporty, fun-loving cousin. He and Pauline epitomized the sixties to me, with Pauline's pixie haircut and their perennial optimism. I felt our Paul was as "fab" as Paul McCartney. They are around the same age.

# CHAPTER 7

# The Ashdown Forest and Pinetree Farm

Much of my childhood was spent exploring the Ashdown Forest—navigating rocky stream beds in my rubber "wellie boots," picking bluebells in the woods, and playing in "pill boxes," small, concrete fortifications left over from World War Two. I often stayed overnight at Debbie's house on the forest's edge and enjoyed playing with her and her little brother, Martyn. Debbie's family always made me feel at home, and her mum allowed us to roam anywhere on the forest as long as we took their sweet boxer dog, Josie, to watch over us.

Debbie and I had many an adventure, pretending to get lost, actually getting lost, and then finding our way home. A crumbling old mill said to have produced the flour for Queen Victoria's wedding cake stood by the stream. Debbie and I enjoyed climbing the mill's precarious, mossy walls and crawling through its damp, mildew-smelling tunnels, with Josie hunting for sticks nearby.

Another friend, Val, lived close by, and her family kindly invited Mum and me on summer day trips to the beach in their car. A day at the beach in Sussex involves briefly swimming in the chilly sea and then running to towel dry as quickly as possible—all good fun and invigorating. Val and I also spent Thursday evenings in her living room watching *Top of the Pops*, a program featuring live performances by bands whose records had made the top twenty. It was crucial to be "with it" in those days, and *Top of the Pops* helped us keep up to date.

*Val, Debby, and I (right to left) at a horse show*

Through Val, I started riding horses, an activity that became my passion and lasted throughout my teen years. Aside from pony rides at village fetes, I had never considered riding a possibility. However, at around eight years old, Val, Debbie, and I took lessons together at Pinetree Farm on the forest's edge.

The farm was owned by Bunty and Tommy Douglas, a wonderfully kind yet no-nonsense couple in their forties, who kept around 30 horses and ponies, an assortment of dogs, two cows, and two goats. We were in awe of Bunty, who drove lorries in Egypt during World War Two and whose cheery authority commanded the respect of everyone in her orbit—two and four-legged. Tommy, mild-mannered, with a delightful sense of humor, was a mathematics teacher and also worked tirelessly on the farm, mending fences and milking his cows when not at work.

We began taking half-hour riding lessons with someone walking beside us, progressing to longer rides following a leader out onto the forest. Before and after riding, we learned to brush and tack up the ponies and helped with feeding, watering, and mucking out the stables. I was nervous around ponies at first but grew to love every minute.

Becoming obsessed with horses, Val, Debbie, and I dragged our families to local agricultural shows to watch show jumping competitions and devoured children's books about ponies and gymkhanas (competitive games on horseback). Val and I staged make-believe gymkhanas in her garden, our bicycles standing in for the ponies. I recall the thrill of attempting to navigate the paths around her dad's immaculate flower beds without falling off my bike or damaging his precious flowers.

# CHAPTER 8

# A First Trip to France

Crowborough lies twenty-five miles north of the English Channel, with France beckoning beyond. While I was at St. John's School, Crowborough was ceremoniously "twinned" with the French town of Montargis. Having inherited Mum's love of all things European, I was excited to learn that a group of students from Montargis would be visiting Crowborough for the summer, staying with host families.

Unfairly, in my opinion, our family didn't qualify as hosts because we didn't have a spare room in our two-bedroom flat. Not to be left out, Val and I hatched a plan whereby I would pretend to be her French guest at the welcome reception at her school. It was perfect—no one knew me there, and I had the brilliant idea of wearing blue socks (everyone knows that only French schoolgirls wear blue socks). It didn't work. Neither the socks nor my limited language skills fooled the teacher at the entrance to the event, although he was somewhat puzzled and conceded that, although not French, I might possibly be German. Our attempt to access the reception was unsuccessful, but fortunately, Debbie's family hosted a student, Marianne, that summer, and we all spent time together.

*Val and I goofing around at a local bus stop*

Mum booked a trip to Paris with her friends the following year, and I was invited. We boarded a bright yellow, 12-seater minivan with Renata, our vivacious European driver and tour guide. By this time, I was used to being with Mum and her friends, some of whom were in their fifties and sixties, and I now joined in their conversations rather than tuning them out. Staying at a budget hotel, in a room whose shutters opened to the busy street below, we delighted in breakfasts of café au lait and croissants with apricot preserves. We wandered around the City of Light, from the height of the Sacre Coeur and Montmartre to the Champs Elysees and Notre Dame. We ate *croque monsieurs* in the Latin Quarter and shopped for prints at nearby tourist booths. Our one splurge was attending a performance at the Opéra Comique. We didn't realize we were supposed to tip the attendant showing us to our seats, resulting in some ruckus and suppressed giggles within our group of middle-aged women.

I loved soaking up the city's atmosphere as we walked for miles, but my new sandals gave me blisters, so I continued barefoot. This appealed to my budding bohemian sensibility, but Mum was less than enthralled. The whole trip felt magical and increased my love of the French language and culture.

# CHAPTER 9

# The Dreaded Eleven-Plus

As I turned 11, the specter of the eleven-plus exam loomed menacingly before me. This was a standardized test to determine the type of secondary education a student would receive, and it has largely been phased out today. It was a big deal to my parents because passing would grant me a free ticket to grammar school and what they deemed a quality education.

I had always been considered creative, somewhat intelligent, if a little dreamy. My parents assumed I'd pass the eleven-plus, but as it drew near, I began to have recurrent dreams that my friends passed and I failed—which is precisely what happened. The exam was confusing. I sat staring at an unfamiliar, multiple-choice paper, taking a stab at the answers but with no clear idea of what I was supposed to be doing—no test preps in those days.

When the pass results were read out in class, I waited hopefully for my name, but it didn't come. Seeing my disappointment, my teacher told me I "did very well," but I was disconsolate. Walking home that afternoon, Debbie saw my dad approaching to meet us and called out,

"Poor Pippi failed her eleven-plus!" Not a high point in my life.

Next was Mum.

"I don't know what we're going to do with you," she said as we walked to the village the next day. Her comment surprised me, but I now understand that she was stating a fact—she *didn't* know what to do with me. At the time, I felt disappointed at her reaction but opted for an encouraging tone.

"Paul failed his eleven-plus, Mummy, and he's done ever-so-well, hasn't he?"

My parents were wary of the local Secondary Modern school, located across from our home, to which I had by default been assigned, although I would have been happy to go there. As it happened, Mum consulted with Val's mum, and it was decided that I'd join Val at Fosse Bank School for Girls, a small and relatively inexpensive private school in Tonbridge, in the county of Kent—an hour's bus ride each way.

Meanwhile, I continued my weekly riding lessons at Pinetree Farm, often staying to help take care of the animals, and was invited into the farmhouse for meals. One evening, I was peeling potatoes in the kitchen when Bunty came in.

"Pip, you're still here. It's getting late. I thought you'd gone home."

"I've almost finished, Bunty. I'm a bit slow. . . maybe being left-handed?" Bunty gave me a big smile.

"Why don't you stay to dinner—stay the night? Go and ring your parents. We'd love to have you."

I called a neighbor, who gave a message to my parents (we still didn't have a phone), and ended up happily staying at the farm, not only that night but most weekends and school holidays over the next six years.

Were those two events connected: my parents' disappointment at my failing the eleven-plus and my focus switching to the farm? I certainly didn't think about it then, but maybe the universe was giving me a nudge—helping me expand my horizons beyond home.

# CHAPTER 10

# Secondary School and Life on the Farm

On turning twelve, I took the double-decker, lime green bus to Fosse Bank School each morning. The classes were okay—the teachers did their best—but I wasn't motivated to study seriously. I made some good friends, though. Wendy owned a couple of ponies, Priscilla and Dylan, and invited me to her home some weekends. I enjoyed riding with her and helping feed her pet hen, Clara Cluck. The main challenge was that Wendy lived even farther away than school. Two other friends, Sandy and Angela, lived in Tunbridge Wells, closer to home, and we rode the bus together each day. I have good memories of Fosse Bank. My classmates and I were together for the entire six years, for the most part, and some of us are still in touch.

Getting off the bus in Crowborough each afternoon, I walked or ran the mile to the farm and started mucking out stables, leading ponies to and from the fields, and, in summer, riding on the forest. At around 7:00 p.m., I walked home, ate the dinner Mum had prepared, and did my homework.

Bunty and Tommy's two children, Hugh and Susie, were two and three years younger than me. There were three full-time grooms, and we all got on well together over the years. I particularly enjoyed thoughtful conversations with Jane, one of the grooms, on Sunday evenings as we pushed our bicycles up the steep hill to the village and our respective homes. In addition to the regulars, there was a constant stream of young people who, like myself, considered Pinetree Farm their second home. Whenever someone new came to the door, we were instructed to offer them a cup of tea and then find out who they were. Everyone, seemingly, was made welcome there.

Staying at the farm most weekends and school holidays, we made sure the ponies were watered and fed each morning before going in for breakfast. The kitchen had a warm and friendly vibe, with breakfasts of toast, various jams and spreads, and lots of tea. Well-behaved dogs napped on a bed in the kitchen corner, and a guinea pig squeaked for cornflakes from a hay-filled cardboard box next to the stove.

After breakfast, Bunty produced a hand-written list with the times of the day's various rides and who was riding which pony. We were always excited to see the list and went out once or twice daily, depending on which animals needed exercising. Sometimes, we accompanied students learning to ride, ensuring everyone kept up and watching out for those needing help. Other times, we rode out as a group, navigating forest paths flanked by bracken, heather, and gorse bushes, sliding down mossy banks to cross streams, and scrambling up the other side. Some tracks had fallen trees to jump over, which was fun for the ponies and us.

On the other side of the stream was a plantation of fir trees, separated by fire breaks that were good for cantering. And even farther was the "top forest," near where my dad worked, where we rode for a couple of hours on Sunday mornings and where we could let the ponies flatten to an exhilarating gallop. No more church for me!

Not everything went according to plan. One day, while cantering in the plantation, we were joined by a herd of deer, spooking the ponies and themselves into a galloping frenzy. Another time, a friend and I raced ponies Ziggy and Frond along a flat path but, unable to stop at the end, careened into a wood, where I slammed into a fallen tree and got my first concussion. And, yes, I did fall off frequently and sometimes spectacularly, for which I was often teased in a good-natured way. Once, at a horse show, I was late for an event about to commence. With everyone nearby urging me to hurry, I jumped onto the pony, Silver, and attempted to ride off, not realizing he was still tied to a tree branch. It took a while to live that one down, and I got used to hearing the phrase "Typical Pip!" I didn't mind as I was, by now, becoming comfortable with my innate quirkiness.

*Debbie and I at a horse show with ponies Fern and William*

One of my English friends at the farm had a guitar, playing folk songs from her *Joan Baez Song Book*. I was fascinated and asked her to show me a few chords. Over time, I acquired a guitar of my own, starting with folk songs and moving on to simple pop songs such as "Leaving on a Jet Plane" and "Spirit in the Sky." My friend and I also invented silly songs about life on the farm. The guitar was a perfect fit for me: I loved to sing; it was a good outlet for my creative energy and was transportable. I have never taken lessons but have been happily strumming and singing along ever since.

# CHAPTER 11

# International Students
# and Horse Shows

Summer at the farm was my favorite season, when international students aged eight to late teens arrived to spend a few weeks there. They came from The Netherlands, Sweden, France, and Switzerland, bringing their unique languages, personalities, and sense of humor. One year, students filled the entire house, so a friend and I slept in bunk beds in a free-standing concrete stable, with a side panel removed to serve as a window. A Swedish student gave me a pair of colorfully patched and faded jeans; another lent me her multi-colored watch for a year. Mostly, the students increased my love of all things international, and I enjoyed practicing my French and learning random phrases in Swedish and Dutch. My favorite Swedish phrase was "Ät mer gröt," "Eat more oatmeal!"

Summer was also horse shows—ranging from local gymkhanas to regional events. On show mornings, we rose before dawn to brush the ponies, plait their manes and tails, and apply bandages to their legs for protection on the trip. After breakfast, we loaded the ponies and ourselves into a horse box (trailer) and were driven to our destination.

Some events were "in hand," where we led ponies around the arena to be judged on how they looked and moved. Other times, we watched Jane, Hugh, and Susie compete in hunter trials and show jumping classes. Gymkhanas were the most fun, and I especially enjoyed competing in the bending, musical sacks, and sack races. The day generally ended with jumping competitions, either Chase Me Charlie—a knock-out contest where one jump is raised higher and higher—or simple show jumping competitions, with a series of low jumps to be navigated. My parents often came to watch, arriving by bus or walking miles along country lanes to reach the showground, and I made time to chat with them, pony in tow, and share a picnic lunch.

Bunty signed us up for a musical ride for one show, and I saw this as a particularly challenging activity. In a musical ride, several horses and riders move in unison, similar to synchronized swimming. You ride around an arena at various paces, to music, splitting up, and coming together again. The list was announced, and I groaned inwardly—I was on Sugar, a pony I felt was about as responsive as a sack of potatoes. After a dismal practice run, I plucked up the courage to request a change.

"Bunty, about the musical ride, I don't think I'll be able to keep up on Sugar. To be honest, I'd rather ride *Shadow*!

"Really? All right, Pip, I'll see what we can do."

If I'd been sincere and less dramatic, I would have asked to ride one of the many responsive and gorgeous ponies on the farm. But I chose to employ sarcasm and name the only animal less attractive than Sugar. The final list was posted, and I was on Shadow, a substantial iron-grey mare with the physique of a cart-horse. She was known to be sluggish and to have a bit of an attitude, but I couldn't complain as my request had been granted. On reflection, I admit that to this day, I'm still hesitant to ask directly for something.

The show was only a few miles away, so we rode there rather than being driven in a horse box. I mounted Shadow, and she was off and running—literally. I couldn't stop her, so I concentrated on steering. Someone must have slipped her a couple of buckets of oats because she rode like a combination of a steamroller and rocket ship all day. We survived the musical ride—it's hard to keep smiling when your leg is constantly being crunched against someone else's as you come together. Next were the competitions: Shadow plowed through the bending race, winning the final at top speed. The musical sack contest was more challenging (think musical chairs with sacks on the ground instead of chairs and a lot of mounting and dismounting). The rest of the afternoon was a blur, culminating in the Chase Me Charlie knockout jumping competition, when Shadow decided she loved jumping, and we came second. At the show's end, Shadow and I were presented with a trophy for best novice horse and rider (okay, a tiny trophy, but the only one I ever won). Thank you, Shadow—you had the last laugh that day!

Another annual event was a hunter trial, which took place on trails throughout a plantation of pine trees. Fixed jumps were located at intervals around the course, and the idea was for individual horses and riders to complete the course within an allotted time. Fixed jumps are tricky because they can't be knocked over, unlike those in show jumping. The first year, I was a spectator, watching Hugh, Susie, Jane, and others compete, and I wondered if I'd ever be able to tackle the novice level.

A year later, I was privileged to ride one of the sweetest and most competent horses, Fielden Small Lord, around the more advanced course. I almost didn't make it because another horse, Glory, kicked me in the inner thigh two days before the event. Bruised and swollen, I couldn't fit into my skinny jodhpurs for the competition, so Bunty lent me her stretch pants. Thanks to Lord, I navigated the jumps with balance and no grip and managed to stay on. We weren't placed, but it didn't matter—getting around that cross-country course was one of the high points of my teenage years. Also, it taught me not to underestimate what's possible in the future based on a current situation. Looking back, I am overwhelmed by the opportunities we were given as kids—Bunty presumably filled out entry forms for the gymkhanas and paid the fees.

*Jumping with Fielden Small Lord*

One day, while steadying a pony as the blacksmith fitted its shoes, he commented that working with animals was the best way to spend my teens. I agreed with him then, but now I understand why: we didn't need to create drama and excitement because we lived it daily. We worked hard, getting up early, often finishing late, and pushing endless wheelbarrows to the muck heap. But there was a strong feeling of camaraderie, belonging, and being appreciated, and we loved being there.

Aside from horse-related activities, we took the vacationing students ice-skating in Brighton, sightseeing in London, and to the cinema in Tunbridge Wells. I don't remember what we saw on one particular occasion, but all fifteen of us decided to run up to Bunty and call her "Mum" while she was buying the tickets—we thought that was hysterical.

Dances were held in one of the farm's barns, and the French students taught us a fast-paced rock 'n roll, which we subsequently took to local disco dance competitions. On seeing us practice, Bunty mused that it was too bad I didn't ride as well as I danced, and she was right—I'm not a naturally relaxed rider, but I've always enjoyed dancing. It was the disco era, after all.

Lastly, the family's Aunt Una owned a swimming pool at her property on the forest, complete with quaint changing huts dating back to a bygone era. After a hot summer's day hay-making in the fields with Tommy or after working in the yard, we piled into the Land Rover and went for a refreshing swim in the slightly murky pool.

I'm not sure how my parents felt about my spending so much time on the farm. Maybe they were relieved I had found something I enjoyed. Did they miss me during the school holidays? I was always happy to see them when they came to horse shows, but otherwise, I rarely saw them during the Summer.

I recall one exception when Mum took me to Paris again when I was 14. One day, I was at a large agricultural show, covered in dust and sweat, caring for the horses. The next day, I was crossing the English Channel by ferry on our way to visit the Louvre, the Luxembourg Gardens, and Fontainebleau Palace. Frank, our minibus driver, took pity on me as the only youngster in Mum's group of friends, escorting me to the top of Notre Dame's bell tower to survey the city. Another memory is of shopping with Mum in Galleries Lafayette, where I purchased one-piece zip-up pajamas in orange toweling. I loved those pajamas and wore them every night—until they fell apart.

*Crossing the English Channel to France*

# CHAPTER 12

# Summer Jobs

Whenever I grew tired of mucking out stables and filling water buckets, I stayed home to visit school friends or shop in Tunbridge Wells. Val and I played tennis at a local club or sunbathed on a flat roof outside her bedroom window, lazily reading magazines and drinking glasses of orange squash with ice cubes.

I also worked a variety of jobs. The first was at age 14, chopping vegetables, dusting furniture, and running errands one summer at the White Hart Hotel, the closest pub to our home. I couldn't understand the strong Sussex accent of one long-term employee, thinking I was supposed to deliver a pork pie to an elderly upstairs resident when he had ordered a port wine. It was an honest mistake, but the resident wasn't happy.

My main Saturday job was at a small health food café close to the Pantiles in Tunbridge Wells. The Pantiles is an elegant, old-fashioned pedestrian walkway lined with quaint shops. Steps at one end lead down to an ancient spring, whose waters are supposed to have medicinal value. I always enjoyed subjecting visiting family and friends to the metallic-tasting water scooped into a communal metal cup chained to the spring's edge—decidedly unhygienic by today's standards. The café where I worked was a short distance from the spring.

Arriving early at my job on Saturday mornings, I shopped for fresh produce at a local market and chopped vegetables for the main rice salad dish. As customers arrived, the café owner and I prepared grilled sandwiches and coffee and served desserts. Sometimes, I'd be alone in the café, and a bus-load of tourists would wander in, which was stressful. The job was fun overall, and I learned a lot. The only problem was that it left just Sunday for the farm.

# CHAPTER 13

# A Teenager's Bedroom and Goodbye to Nan

A teenager's bedroom is a refuge from the adult world, a reflection of her personality, and a place to express creativity. I tried to make my room look hip, with a black and white stereo record player next to my bed and my Rod Stewart, Elton John, and David Bowie vinyl albums. Posters and postcards from faraway places decorated the walls, which I painted sky blue. There was nothing to be done about the mangle, however. A what, you may ask? Mum did the laundry by hand, so after washing clothes, she put them through the mangle's two rollers, turning a hand crank to squeeze the water into a bucket. She then hung the clothes out to dry. In our flat, the only space for the mangle, which I painted white to match my record player, was in my room.

Also, Dad refused to have the TV (we now had one that worked) in the living room, calling it the "bloody box," so it was consigned to my room. I watched *Morecambe and Wise* and *Cilla* on Saturday evenings and spent many a Friday night trying to stay awake to *Monty Python's Flying Circus*. Mum preferred old films, spending weekend afternoons sitting on my bed watching Jimmy Stewart, Gregory Peck, and her other

Hollywood heart-throbs. She also enjoyed an early morning show called *Make Yourself at Home*, created for newly arrived Pakistani immigrants. When home, I often awoke to the sound of elaborate song and dance routines—presumably in Urdu, with Mom perched on the end of my bed, swaying to the music. Dad overcame his disdain for the TV enough to stop by for *Star Trek* one evening per week. I remember him welling up with emotion at one particularly satisfying conclusion.

The spare bed in my room was used by Nan, Auntie Elsie, or whoever was visiting. One year, when Nan was 84, she came to stay but went straight to bed, saying she was feeling poorly. Aside from a few mouthfuls of fish, she hardly ate or drank anything, and Mum asked me to sleep on the living room sofa when it became apparent that Nan would soon pass. I listened through the crack in my bedroom door while she instructed Mum not to throw away her knitted dresses and jackets, and Nan died that night. At school the next day, I thought about telling Mrs. Cardin why I only got 13 out of 20 on my French vocabulary test but decided not to. I loved Nan and missed her immensely. An ardent Beatles fan, she owned most of their records and magazines, and her passing coincided with the time the Beatles split up. I'm glad she spent her last days with us rather than alone, and I still feel that she's not far away.

# CHAPTER 14

# Christmas

My room was also where Mum steamed our Christmas pudding over a paraffin (kerosene) stove in my Victorian fireplace grate. Going to sleep to the bubbling of water and the warm scent of fruit and spice, with a whiff of paraffin mixed in, was enchanting—especially with the promise of Christmas the next day.

Christmas was quiet when I was little, spent with Mum, Dad, and Nan at home. I was always excited on Christmas Eve and couldn't sleep. Concerned that Father Christmas didn't visit children who were awake, I had a pressing question:

"Mummy, do people sleep with their mouths open or closed?

"Open, I think, Dear. Why?"

That was all I needed. I spent what seemed like hours the night of Christmas Eve lying in bed, my mouth stretched uncomfortably wide, just in case. The next morning, a pillowcase containing a few gifts lay at the bottom of my bed, so I wasn't concerned about tricking Father Christmas in subsequent years.

Christmas and Boxing Day from around age eleven were delightful. Christmas morning was spent quietly with my parents, eating lunch together, after which I rode my bicycle to the farm. We worked with the horses until early evening and then gathered in the kitchen, where Bunty served a turkey dinner with stuffing and roast potatoes. After dinner, we crammed into the living room, around a crackling log fire, and opened presents. We all received several gifts—simple, practical, and inexpensive—but each was wrapped and a surprise. The TV played whatever special was on, and boxes of chocolates and Dutch Spekulatius (almond windmill cookies) were passed around.

On Boxing Day, our extended family came to visit. By that time, Paul and Pauline had two young children, Matt and Vivian, and Christine had a young son, Gareth. With Auntie Elsie, we ate turkey sandwiches, followed by Mum's trifle doused with sherry, and marzipan-covered Christmas cake topped with snow-white icing. I had previously shopped for everyone's gifts in Crowborough, and these were placed around a small, pine-scented Christmas tree. After opening presents, we lit indoor fireworks that sputtered to life from a tray on our living room table. In retrospect, the fireworks were smoky and underwhelming, but the youngsters thought them riveting, and their enthusiasm was contagious. Mum was always in top form, joking and entertaining everyone. I played my guitar, and we sang songs, played charades, and thoroughly enjoyed ourselves.

# CHAPTER 15

# Walking Along Country Lanes

Without a family car, my early years were spent walking—to school, bus stops, and the farm. There were also long walks on the forest with my parents or friends. Walking or running was my primary means of getting around unless I rode my bike.

At some point in my teens, though, I began walking alone for no particular reason, and walking in the countryside became my way of inviting clarity for the future. Following a footpath opposite the White Hart pub, I passed the secondary school, arriving at a stream crossing my path. I enjoyed sitting on the stream's dirt bank, watching light playing on the water as it splashed over pebbles, daydreaming about nothing in particular. Farther on was a wood, carpeted with bluebells in season, and, past the wood, I crossed a lane and climbed over a stile into a field. At some point, before it got dark, I headed home.

Walking in the countryside or by water has always balanced and connected me, and I still walk almost daily. I love being in the moment, alert to the rhythm of my pace, the rustle of leaves, birdsong, and light filtering through trees. Alternatively, in a neighborhood, appreciating the diversity of passers-by and quietly acknowledging old folk, mothers with children, and dogs. I enjoy checking out local shops, restaurants, and farmers' markets, chatting with neighbors, and purchasing something when needed.

Walking is so important to me; I decided to give it a chapter of its own! Now, back to the story.

*A countryside memory with Mum*

# CHAPTER 16

# The Disco Era

Reaching my mid-teens, I started going to pubs and discos locally with farm friends or, more frequently, joining school friends in Tunbridge Wells. The latter was problematic because the last bus for the eight-mile ride home to Crowborough was at 10:20 p.m. My school friend Sandy often kindly let me stay at her house, but transportation was an ongoing challenge.

I tried the local Crowborough Teen & Twenty club at All Saints Church, mostly comprised of 14 – 17-year-olds. After a few meetings there, a boy invited me to a "coffee squash" event in a neighboring town. I had always enjoyed playing squash (like racquetball), so I happily met him for the walk to the bus, racquet in hand. It soon became apparent that coffee squash had nothing to do with the game. Instead, we would "squash" into someone's home and drink coffee. Mortified, I left my racquet at the bus stop, mumbling the improbable excuse that I was dropping it off for someone to pick up later. The event was fine, as Christian gatherings go, but I didn't return to Teen & Twenty again.

Tunbridge Wells, larger than Crowborough, had more options for entertainment, and my friends and I enjoyed dances at The Elizabethan

Barn there. Aside from a disc jockey providing classic rock music, I remember pickle-eating contests and a race that involved sitting on boys' shoulders and climbing over a succession of the barn's rafters. I've always loved a challenge!

The Court School of Dancing offered traditional ballroom dances, and my school friends and I gave these a whirl for a time. One memorable event was the "Decimal Day Dance," on or around February 15th, 1971, when the United Kingdom changed its currency from pounds, shillings, and pence to the decimal system of 100 pence, or p, to the pound. On entering the dance hall, with our spiky short haircuts and "hot pants" shorts (a fashion phase that, mercifully, was short-lived), we were each presented with a plastic pouch containing smaller denominations of the new currency. This was exciting to me, as I longed to be European.

Sandy and I tried another discotheque above a wine bar called The Streets of London. The upstairs floor of the old building bounced as we danced—structurally discomforting and memorable. I danced with a boy who, at the end of the evening, invited Sandy and me to a nearby pub called The Compasses, where we met his friends. This group of 18-year-old lads had left school at 16 and were either working or were apprenticed to a trade. Soon after, we brought our school friends to meet them, and we all got together socially for the next several years.

I enjoyed hanging out with this group—visiting various pubs, going on trips to the beach, or boating on a local river. We had many laughs, and the lads I dated were exceptionally kind and considerate. I appreciated the friendship of our entire group but was not ready for a long-term exclusive relationship or settling down at that point in my life. Still skinny and behind the developmental curve in my teens, I wasn't interested in marriage or sex, aside from a vague romantic notion. On reflection, I probably should have been more upfront about not looking for a "steady boyfriend," as we used to say, although I'm not sure I was aware of that then.

# CHAPTER 17

# O-Levels and a Visit to the Scottish Isles

As I neared sixteen, it was time for O-levels—the standardized tests following the eleven-plus, generally taken in 4 – 8 subjects. This time, I was ready! I studied on the front lawn of Craigmore Hall in the June sunshine, reading textbooks and taking notes, while Mum clattered comfortingly around in the kitchen above (we had moved down to the second floor by then).

My O-level results came that summer while I was on holiday with Mum and Dad in the Shetland Islands. I hadn't been anywhere with my parents for a while, and it was a chance to see somewhere new, so I went along. The Shetlands are the most northerly Islands in Great Britain, and we stayed in Unst, the most northern island in the Shetlands—the nearest main post office was in Bergen, Norway. We took a train to Aberdeen, Scotland, followed by a choppy overnight voyage north by ship to the main Shetland town of Lerwick. We then boarded a smaller boat to the tiny island of Unst, finding our guest house in the village of Baltasound. A fence surrounding the village kept the wild Shetland ponies out, but the rest of the island was theirs to roam.

Standing on the rocky shore outside our lodgings on our first evening, I contemplated—with a mixture of awe and disappointment—how remote the island was. After a few minutes, a guest house employee arrived, waving a phone message from a neighbor in Crowborough. I had passed my O-levels in 8 subjects with good grades. I looked out to sea with an uncommon feeling of satisfaction, contemplating my future, before heading back and being congratulated by my parents and the other guests—all six of them.

Wildlife on the island was plentiful. We saw puffins, seals, skewers (birds that attack their prey by swooping down in a corkscrew motion), and a snowy owl. Mum and I found a row boat, but it started to sink as soon as we attempted to push it out, so that didn't work. I was saved from dying of teenage boredom by a bicycle I rode around the island daily.

On arriving at the northern tip, I assumed there would at least be somewhere to get ice cream or a postcard to commemorate the geographic location of the northernmost point in the British Isles. Instead, I was greeted by desolate moorland, with cliffs dropping off to waves crashing on rocks below. After a few minutes, I was startled by a droning noise that increased to a deafening roar as a squadron of fighter planes passed low overhead before receding into the distance. I later learned there was a NATO base nearby. I'm glad I went on that trip but wrote in my journal, somewhat dramatically, that it would be the last time I went on holiday with my parents—and it was.

# CHAPTER 18

# Studying Languages

My O-level grades would have allowed me to transfer to the Tunbridge Wells Grammar School to join those who had passed their eleven-plus—revenge at last! I could have taken A-levels there and continued to university, and I briefly contemplated that path.

Instead, I enrolled in a secretary linguist program at West Kent College, also in Tunbridge Wells. There, I could focus on languages and wear jeans and a tee shirt rather than another wretched school uniform, which the Grammar School would have required.

The United Kingdom had been moving toward entry into the European Economic Community and officially joined in January 1973, coinciding with my studies at West Kent. It was an exciting time, as doggedly monolingual England now needed people who could speak European languages. There was an optimistic feeling of expansion, of going beyond borders, and my newly chosen course of study made me feel part of the action.

I initially took German as my second language, having studied it at Fosse Bank, but was soon drawn to Spanish instead. Not wanting to waste time, I pretended I had already completed a year of Spanish, enrolling in the intermediate class. Mrs. Lopez, my long-suffering lecturer, wasn't fooled for one minute and wrote, *This is not second-year work!* in red ink on my first assignment, but I studied hard and caught up quickly.

Ever the dreamer, I saw two spheres hovering slightly above eye level to my right, one representing French and the other Spanish. The spheres were beautiful and complete, and I felt as if I already knew both languages—I just had to fill in the centers. From that point on, I was focused on that goal. Each morning, I awoke to the French language radio station *Europe 1*, absorbing the words to both the pop songs and the commercials. One commercial I recall featured a dramatic roar, followed by the phrase *Mammouth écrase les prix!* (Mammoth hypermarket crushes prices).

I acquired a moped—a tiny motorcycle with a 50cc engine and pedals, favored by French schoolchildren who could ride them at age 14. My "putt-putt," as Bunty called it, enabled me to get around Crowborough more efficiently but wasn't reliable for longer trips, as I still had to pedal uphill. I then traded the moped for a Honda 70cc, a little more powerful with no pedals, which freed me up somewhat, although the constant English rain and fog didn't help. I now wonder why I didn't save for a car, especially as I passed my driving test at seventeen.

A college grant from West Kent provided enough money for tuition, books, and other necessities. At that time, Bunty and Tommy acquired a contract to clean the brand-new Waitrose supermarket in Crowborough to help with expenses. Several of us from the farm pitched in, cleaning weekday mornings from 7:00 – 8:30 a.m. Stopping by the bakery after work, I picked up a sausage roll and a doughnut and then hopped on the bus to college. The job provided extra cash without my having to work Saturdays, and the cleaning workout energized me for class, aided by the bakery boost.

Mornings at West Kent consisted of shorthand, typing, and administrative skills—not my favorite subjects, but I was up for the challenge of speed tests, and keyboarding has been handy throughout my life. Afternoons were French, Spanish, international commerce, and sociology. The lecturers were interesting, and I enjoyed hearing about their life experiences along with the subject matter. One older lecturer, Mrs. Moncrief, spoke about her life in France and New York in a charming French-American accent.

I enjoyed the freedom of college, the extra cash my grant and job provided, and the relative mobility offered by my little Honda 70. These were good years!

PART 2

# FRANCE AND SPAIN

# CHAPTER 19

# Staying With the Lavignes

Toward the end of my first year at West Kent, a lecturer asked if I'd be interested in spending the summer with a family in northern France. "Yes, absolutely, thank you! When do I leave?"

The Lavigne family consisted of Monsieur, Madame, and their five children, aged 14 to 28. The three younger siblings lived with their parents in a small, semi-detached house in the hills above Rouen, and the older sons came over for meals. Madame made extra cash providing daycare for two babies, and Monsieur was a postal worker, as I recall. I shared a room with Fabienne, who was close to my age, and I mostly hung out with her and her younger brother, Lucien.

It took me a day or so to understand their accent in French. On my first evening, Lucien asked if I liked what I heard as *spur*. I had no idea what he was talking about.

"*Spur*, you know, like football," he clarified (the pronunciation I was accustomed to would be more like "*spor*"). Once we had that figured out, I was up and running, and we always spoke French. Looking back, I was probably there to help improve their English, but that didn't occur to me then.

Fabienne was super-intelligent, compassionate, and unstoppable. She was also aware of societal and racial issues. Having suffered from polio as a child, she was willowy thin and wore a back brace. Fabienne also played the guitar and taught me folk and protest songs, along with pop songs in both French and Spanish. We both had a thing for the pop star Julio Iglesias, with his emotional, romantic ballads.

Lucien, 14, was more laid back. Fun-loving and a typical teenager, he taught me French slang, curse words, and tongue twisters. Fabienne, Lucien, and I wandered around their small town of Mont-Saint-Aignan, visiting cafes and hanging out with their friends. In contrast to my busy life on the farm, I delighted in perfecting the art of being a bored French teenager during those hot summer days. Our teen magazines of choice were *Mademoiselle Age Tendre* for girls and *Salut les Copains* for boys, from which I upgraded my knowledge of the European pop scene.

*Acting cool in Mont-Saint-Aignan*

We ate around a large rectangular table with a red and white checkered tablecloth, and I became accustomed to drinking wine and ending each meal with cheese. Madame educated me about the *Trou Normand*—meaning that people from Normandy always have room for a good camembert or brie after a meal. I couldn't bring myself to eat *boudin* (blood sausage) but was open to most delicacies of the region. I loved being part of this big, boisterous family of seven.

Weekends were reserved for trips. We visited Normandy beaches, collecting mussels in a bucket in the seaside town of Deauville. We paid our respects at Second World War battlefields and graveyards, where hundreds of white crosses mark the burial sites of British and North American service members. Wandering around the narrow medieval streets of Rouen, Fabienne showed me the 14th-century astrological clock, known as the *Gros-Horloge*, and took me to Joan of Arc Square, where the 19-year-old was burned at the stake in 1431, later becoming canonized as Saint Joan.

I returned to the Lavignes several times over the next few years—accompanying Fabienne to high school before her Spring break and attending a secretarial school in Rouen for three weeks. Riding the bus into town for classes by myself each day, I enjoyed trying on my French identity and feeling like it fit.

One year, a Tunisian exchange student was also staying with the Lavignes. I recall Ahmed showing us how to make the most delicious couscous I've ever tasted, prepared in a two-layer pot called a *couscousière*. Fabienne and I also went on a camping trip to Spain (more of that later), and she and Lucien visited me in England. I've lost touch with this wonderful family from my teen years, but I would love to reconnect.

# CHAPTER 20

# Internship in Paris

During Spring break of my second college year, a classmate and I were offered a three-week internship in Paris at the *Maisons Internationales de la Jeunesse et des Etudiants* (MIJE for short), an international student organization. We took a ferry to Dieppe, then a train to Paris, where I was promptly pick-pocketed at the Saint Lazare station, losing most of my cash. Staying in Paris with little money was challenging as, back then, it didn't seem feasible to secure replacement funds from home. Emma and I shared a room in a cheap hotel and worked as receptionists at the MIJE, receiving visitors and answering phone calls in the hectic office.

My saving grace was a complimentary three-course lunch at work each day. Everyone, from interns to management, sat around a large table eating delicious food with wine and then had time to walk it off before heading back to work.

Wandering around in the Spring rain on weekends, we visited one or two museums and took in spectacular views from the top of the newly constructed Montparnasse Tower. Overall, this Paris experience could have been much better, but I was only 18 and mostly trying to make it through each workday with as few mistakes as possible.

Back in England, I spent more time at home, studying, listening to my record collection—having discovered Joni Mitchell and Linda Ronstadt—and going out with friends and the farm crew. I still helped out on the farm when I had time and still loved the sweet animals with their unique individual personalities and quirks, but I was starting to realize that a future with horses was, ultimately, not for me.

# CHAPTER 21

# Summer in Switzerland

That summer, another classmate and I headed to Switzerland for two months, taking turns to work the reception booth at a children's summer camp high in the Alps. We flew to Geneva, took a train through a picturesque valley, then a bus up into the mountains. The air was pristine, scented with pine trees, and the alpine landscape was gorgeous. The job, however, was less than enthralling, and the six hours spent in the reception booth each day seemed to drag.

I shouldn't complain—some aspects were enjoyable. We skated on an ice rink and watched hockey games there. We drove up into the mountain peaks, with their awe-inspiring scenery and views of Mont Blanc. We sampled local delicacies, including fondue and raclette, a tangy alpine melted cheese, which was my favorite.

It wasn't long before I figured out what was bothering me—the disparity between the treatment of native Swiss and northern European staff versus that of workers from other countries who, seemingly, did not fare as well. I was invited to a party where fresh cream pastries were served one night. I was about to bite into mine when a food fight broke out, with eclairs and cream puffs joyfully hurled around the room. I remember making a feeble effort to get into it but felt stunned at the waste. When the party was over, I started to clean up but was told not to worry and that the workers would take care of it.

Deciding to stay for the clean-up operation anyway, I met several Italian and Spanish workers, who invited me to a party with them the following evening. The festivities involved sharing a watermelon and singing songs to a guitar. I knew whose company I preferred.

A nasty stomach bug went through the camp one week later—we're talking about hundreds of kids. I was told to summon the Spanish workers to clean up the infirmary after they had finished their shift. I hesitated, which was unacceptable, and things went downhill from there. Some money from petty cash went missing, and I was held responsible. The money was taken from my pay, but I didn't care—I was happy to get out of there.

I had planned to go straight home after Switzerland, but Marina, a friend from the farm, was spending the summer house-sitting a villa in the hills above Monte Carlo and invited me to join her. On the way there, I spent an afternoon in Geneva walking around a beautiful lakeside park overlooking the famous *Jet d'Eau* fountain and then took a train to Marseille. It was evening in the port town, so I decided to see a movie, *Alice Doesn't Live Here Anymore*, showing in Spanish, rather than wandering alone. After the movie, I boarded the train, located a compartment with a woman passenger and her young daughter for safety, and settled for the journey.

Needing to use the bathroom mid-trip, I slid the compartment door open. Two choices: to walk a longer distance to my right, where there were few people, or to walk a short distance to my left, where there were some sailors. Rationalizing, naively, that I had the right to use whichever bathroom I chose, I headed in the direction of the sailors. The toilet was occupied, so I waited outside, staring at the door, trying to ignore the charged atmosphere around me. The door opened, and I was suddenly shoved hard from behind into the small bathroom, with the sailor who had been about to leave in front of me and another one behind. Instinctively, I thrust my right leg back to block the door from being shut and instantaneously felt a shooting pain as the door closed on my shin. In the tiny space, my face was pressed against the shirted chest of the sailor in front, so—I bit him. There was a shouting of curses, the door opened, and I stumbled out. Heading back to my compartment, with hot, angry tears erupting, I glanced up at a sailor in officer's uniform leaning casually against the carriage wall. "*Faut pas pleurer, Mademoiselle*" (No need to cry, Miss) was his comment. I found my way back to the carriage and remained there for the rest of the journey.

This was the first in a series of over a half dozen incidents experienced in Southern Europe during the mid-to-late seventies. Each was a surprise, requiring a different, quick-thinking response. After the initial shock of each assault, I tended to shake them off and move on. Maybe I viewed them as the price for traveling alone, as obstacles to be overcome on any worthwhile quest. It's also possible that they affected me more than I was willing to admit. I acknowledge that some of my decisions weren't the smartest, but back then, I didn't understand why I attracted attention, dressed in jeans and tee shirts, with no make-up. Suffice it to say that nothing was going to stop me from traveling.

The Mediterranean sparkled in the morning sun as the train pulled into Monte Carlo in the tiny country of Monaco. I took a taxi into the nearby mountains to find Marina in a cozy villa overlooking the sea. Marina is a sweetheart—outspoken, multi-national, sensitive, and funny. She took me to the beach, where we swam, lazed in the sand, and ate *pain bagnats*—delicious rolls filled with tomatoes, anchovies, onions, and olives, all bathed in olive oil. Marina got me a job waitressing at a busy Lowe's Hotel café, where she worked, and I joined her, taking orders and rushing back and forth between tables and the somewhat frantic kitchen. We wore scratchy yellow and orange uniforms to complement the garden theme of the café.

Maybe I was exhausted from my Swiss experience or starting to miss home. It had been an enjoyable visit at the end of a long summer, but I quit the job after a short while, said goodbye to my good friend, and headed back to England.

# CHAPTER 22

# My Last College Year, and Lucy

The Secretary Linguist program was initially for two years, but a third year was added, culminating in a Bi-lingual Secretarial Diploma. Eight students stayed on for this new program, and I looked forward to being in a concentrated learning environment.

Mostly living at home to study, I became good friends with my neighbor, Lucy Fairfax. Ten years older than me, Lucy had lived in the gardener's cottage at the entrance to Craigmore Hall since I was ten, and she was twenty. Tall and strongly built, with long blond hair, Lucy had a good sense of humor and was unfailingly kind. She had a sweet West Highland terrier named Cara, a cat named Nitty Gritty, and a boyfriend named Geoff. A former agricultural student, she loved animals and, at one point, kept chickens at Craigmore Hall, much to the delight of local foxes. She hoped, one day, to own a sheep farm in Wales and was later able to fulfill her dream.

Now that I was 18 and Lucy 28, we spent time together, drinking tea in her cottage, shopping in Tunbridge Wells or Brighton, and sunbathing on the lawn in summer with Cara and Nitty Gritty close by. Lucy also enjoyed Mum's company and was probably with her more than I was during my teens and early twenties. They enjoyed watching the Wimbledon tennis tournament on TV together. Dad was starting to become unsteady when returning from the pub at night, so Lucy kept an eye out for him as he ambled from the main road, along the driveway, and past her cottage. She told us he was our responsibility once he turned the corner near our front door.

*Lucy with Cara and Nitty Gritty*

In addition to trips with Lucy, I became more interested in visiting London—an hour or so by train. I shopped for flared jeans, tie-dye tee shirts, and posters in Kensington Market (it was the seventies, after all). After roaming the Tate Gallery's modern art collection, I started creating abstract art pieces, which joined the posters on my walls. I enjoyed my days in London, wandering around Chinatown, Carnaby Street, and other tourist spots.

For my last Spring break, I enrolled at a London employment agency that placed linguists in temporary secretarial and translating jobs. Becoming friends with the two young women who ran the agency, I worked for them whenever I was low on funds, commuting from Crowborough by train. Most assignments lasted a few weeks, while others were as short as a couple of hours when I was driven to Heathrow Airport or a hotel to translate at business meetings (no Skype or Zoom back then).

# CHAPTER 23

# Belgium and Northern Spain

As my time at West Kent ended, I felt a delicious sense of freedom and possibility. There was no graduation ceremony, just warm exchanges of goodbyes and thanks with the lecturers and a drink at the local pub with classmates.

I began the summer staying with Auntie Elsie in Brighton and appreciated getting to know her better now that I was older. Elsie had taken up oil painting in retirement, and I slept in her art studio, a former family bedroom. Riding my Honda 70 there, I enrolled in an agency that sent me to nearby Sussex University to work in the office of a certain Professor Duchene.

There was no sign of the good professor for several days, but there were constant phone calls for him, and I duly took messages. One caller kept saying, "Professor Duchene," and I kept explaining that he wasn't there. Then the caller erupted, "I am Professor Duchene!" commenting that he felt as if he were in a *Monty Python* skit. So, he did exist, after all.

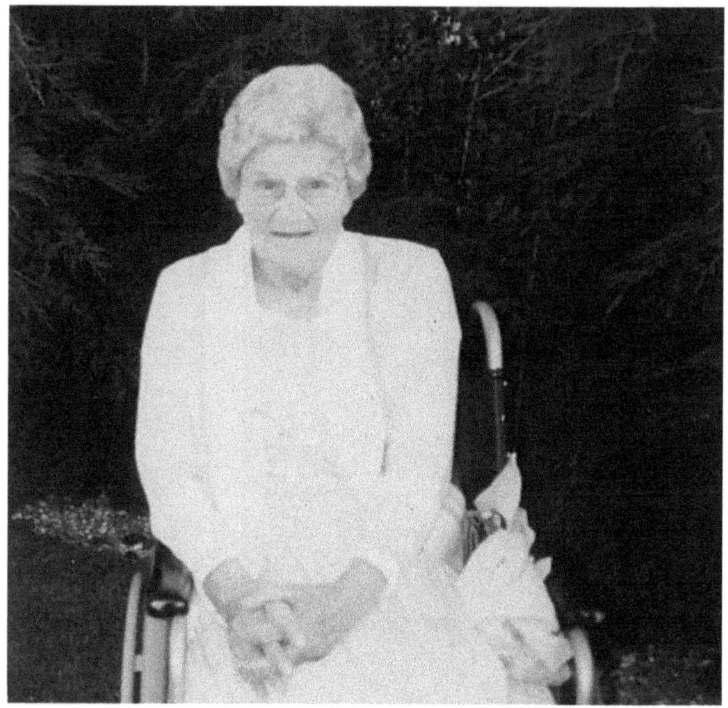

*Elsie later in life*

By then, Bunty and Tommy knew I wasn't planning a career with horses but asked if I wouldn't mind working on the farm for two weeks that summer while the other grooms were away. I happily accepted, organizing work in the yard and helping with the international students during what turned out to be my last consistent period there, although I visited many times subsequently.

Belgium was next on my summer list. Another friend from the farm, Sasha, invited me to stay with her family near Brussels, so I hopped onto a ferry from Dover to Ostend. I spent the night in the Belgian ferry terminal, my legs wrapped around my guitar so it wouldn't get stolen. I have good memories of that trip, helping Sasha care for her ponies, and attending a Cat Stevens concert with her family. Yusuf Cat Stevens is one of my favorite musicians, and it was delightful to see him perform with his guitar, backed by a lively band.

I'd been temping mainly to save for my first trip to Spain that summer—camping near the northern town of Santander. Fabienne was waiting for me at her home near Rouen and had prepared a backpack for herself and a small tent for us both. She reminded me that she couldn't carry either far due to back weakness resulting from her polio but assured me we'd be okay since we'd mostly be taking trains and buses. I admired her confidence, feeling just slightly annoyed as I attempted to pick up our gear. We set off via train to Paris, transferring to another overnight train heading toward the Pyrenees Mountains and Spain.

It's fair to say that not much planning went into that trip. We had a piece of paper with the address of a campsite in Santander, and that was it. After dragging our stuff across the Basque city of San Sebastian, we finally located the bus for the three-hour ride to Santander. The campsite was high on spectacular cliffs amid pine trees, overlooking the sea, and was abuzz with young Spaniards, who kept asking if we had come for the festival.

Some political background might help here. General Francisco Franco, fascist dictator of Spain for 40 years since the Civil War, was ailing during the summer of 1975 and would die that November. There was much political unrest that summer, and groups of more than eight were prohibited in the streets. Fabienne and I weren't clued into this, nor did we realize that the festival was a political protest event. We happily joined a group singing to a guitar around a campfire. We drank wine from *botas* (goatskin bags with a spout) passed around the circle while relaxing and enjoying the music late into the night.

The following evening, the festival was raided by police amid much confusion and scattering, and some individuals were arrested.

Fortunately, it was evident that Fabienne and I were clueless visitors, so we returned to our tent without incident.

Another memory from that trip is swimming in a picturesque bay in Santander. The water was warm, and I swam beyond the breakers, where endless gentle waves rolled in. My previous experience of sea bathing was quick dips in the chilly English Channel, so these warm waves were a whole new experience and mesmerizing. Eventually emerging from my aquatic reverie, I returned to Fabienne, who wasn't into swimming, at the campsite.

On our return trip, we spent a day in the historic city of San Sebastian, climbing the ancient ramparts overlooking the bay, before boarding a train back to France, where I said goodbye to Fabienne and carried on to England.

# CHAPTER 24

# My First Real Job

Back in Crowborough, it was time to look for a real job rather than working for a couple of months and then taking off somewhere—that was the plan, at least. I applied to a translation agency run by a multi-lingual Welshman in the tiny village of Cousley Wood, ten miles from home. I'm not sure why I chose to stay near home for my first full-time job—maybe I needed a rest from traveling, or perhaps working as a translator sounded enticing. I started at Linguatech, riding my Honda 70 along winding country lanes when the weather allowed and getting a ride from a co-worker when it rained hard or snowed.

Each week, the half dozen employees and I translated press releases featuring new products from Europe. Working on blurbs about cosmetics and toiletries was stimulating and fun. I mainly translated from French or Spanish, but sometimes Mr. Matthews, my boss, would hand me something in Portuguese or Italian (a shelf full of multi-lingual technical dictionaries came in handy). Mr. Matthews was kind and patient, often reviewing our work and offering suggestions for improvement as necessary.

We also translated business letters, brochures, and technical documents into English (native European employees were on hand to translate into their languages). With no computers and no internet, work was sent via telex—a cumbersome machine relaying documents over the phone via punched holes in a paper tape.

My co-workers and I occasionally lunched at a nearby pub. More often, though, I ate a packed lunch in the office and then walked around peaceful country lanes between fields. As mentioned before, walking for me means daydreaming, which is rather dangerous because I start imagining new paths for my life.

Mum kindly had dinner ready for me each evening: shepherd's pie, liver and bacon, or sausage and mash, followed by treacle pudding or bread-and-butter pudding. In my spare time, I read Simone de Beauvoir, Camus, Solzhenitsyn, and Sylvia Plath, among others, incorporating a certain degree of angst into my worldview as befitting a now twenty-year-old. Here are the lyrics to a song I wrote around that time:

## With Help from You

There are times when I long to own a sports car
Like those trendy girls in town
Loaded with Biba bags and wearing Yves Saint-Laurent
It all helps to keep the blues down

There are times when I long to find a husband
Raise a child and keep house frantically
Well, it might work out, and, there again, it might not
But at least I'd have some identity

But right now, all I want is my freedom
To learn to love as I choose
Explore the earth and explore our minds

And I can do it with help from you

You see, the search for life can get depressing
And sometimes I feel so far from home
So many questions and so few answers
It's hard to face them all alone

If you ask too much, you lose your balance
And topple over into the bell jar
Where the absurd world outside terrifies you
So, you sit and shiver right where you are

But I know if I ever stop looking
Stop feeling, stop singing, stop crying
I know if I ever give up my search for life
Part of me will be dying

So right now, all I want is my freedom
To learn to love as I choose
Explore the earth and explore our minds
And I can do it with help from you

One of many songs and poems I wrote during my late teens and early twenties, "With Help from You," isn't directed to a specific person but refers to the inner presence I've always sensed—the universal "you," if that makes sense.

Back on planet Earth, Spring rolled around, and I was assigned a 500-page manual from French to English on constructing a Tunisian cement factory—compelling stuff. The project took forever, and I started to get restless. Those lunchtime walks along country lanes became increasingly essential.

As I walked, I thought about how I'd never been to an actual university, as opposed to a community college, and how I'd love to return to Spain. Then I thought how ridiculous that was since I'd been working for less than a year. Stuck in this conundrum, I called Mrs. Moncrief, my lecturer from college, and asked if I could visit for advice.

Mrs. Moncrief lived with her husband in Tunbridge Wells and welcomed me with tea. She had always seemed broad-minded and well-traveled, inserting snippets of her life in Europe and America into her classes. I don't remember much about the meeting other than that by the time I hugged her goodbye (decidedly un-English), I had decided to study in Spain for a year.

I hurried home to mail requests for college brochures and soon had several to choose from, settling on the University of Málaga. Why there? It's on the Costa del Sol, sunny and hot. Also, I had recently seen *A Touch of Class*, in which Glenda Jackson and George Segal's characters spend a weekend in Marbella, down the coast from Málaga. Lastly, I was fascinated with James Michener's book *The Drifters* about young people during the sixties in Torremolinos, next to Málaga. That was it! As you can see, much research went into choosing the right academic location.

There were still several months before I was due to leave for Spain. Mum took French evening classes locally, and her instructor invited me to perform French and Spanish songs with my guitar at an international program she ran in another town. This was my first time playing for people I didn't know, and I enjoyed singing the various songs I had learned with Fabienne to the small but appreciative audience.

Gaining confidence, I joined an Arts Workshop program in Crowborough, where musicians and artists met in the back room of a pub each week. I played my European songs, with enough English folk bal-lads mixed in to enable me to perform at folk evenings at other local pubs. In retrospect, taking guitar and voice lessons would have made sense, but I didn't think about that then. Instead, I listened to Joan Baez's more recent, contemporary songs and tried to copy her finger-picking sequences. To this day, I still don't read music, relying on a basic style I've picked up over the years.

A young married couple from the Arts Workshop invited me to their home for dinners and conversation, and I appreciated spending time with them. Mostly, I was looking forward to leaving for Spain, and that day finally came in September 1976, the month I turned twenty-one.

# CHAPTER 25

# Málaga

A wave of nervous excitement ran through my body as the plane banked over the Mediterranean to land at Málaga Airport. Exiting the terminal, I was met by intense sunlight and the realization that this was somewhere totally new. Málaga is an ancient port city with a Roman amphitheater and an imposing Moorish fortress, the *Alcazaba*. Along the seafront runs a wide boulevard, the *Paseo del Parque*, with a shaded park on each side, where parrots squawk from palm trees. I would come to love this sunny, compact city, but right then, I needed to take a bus into town and walk north to find my lodgings on *Calle Cristo*.

The University had arranged a place for me to stay, and I imagined lodging with a family, similar to the Lavignes in France or Bunty and Tommy's farm. I hauled my backpack and guitar up two flights of stairs to the flat and was surprised to be greeted by a tiny woman in her eighties. Doña Concha was assisted by Dolores, her maid of many years, who was not much younger than she was. The small, three-bedroom flat, I learned, would also house two other lodgers—Isabel, a 17-year-old pre-med student with whom I was to share a room, and Pedro, a math teacher in his thirties.

Soon after my arrival, Pedro took me for an introductory stroll around town, instructing me to always walk on the shady side of the street and treating me to a vino de Málaga, the local sweet fortified wine served in a small glass. Pedro also guided me around the historic district, with its cathedral that's missing a tower, and showed me how to get to the nearby liberal arts department of the university, where my classes would be held.

Pedro's kindness notwithstanding, the flat felt claustrophobic—the room Isabel and I were to share adjoined the living room, where Doña Concha watched soap operas on a loop. The tiny kitchen was Dolores's domain. Despite apparent aches and pains, the round-faced, ever-cheerful Delores took good care of us, serving us *migas* (fried breadcrumbs) for breakfast, *albondigas* (meatballs) for lunch, and a special chicken and seafood paella on Sundays. Delores reminded me of a female Sancho Panza, whereas Doña Concha was more like a female Don Quijote—in appearance, at least. The flat's one redeeming feature was a roof-top patio with chairs and potted plants, where I relaxed and studied in the mornings before it got too hot.

Isabel, my roommate, arrived a couple of days after me. She was bright and chatty, and we got on well enough, but the Faculty of Medicine she attended was on the other side of town, so I didn't see her often. My classes were from 4 – 7 pm daily, a 20-minute walk from the flat, down Calle Cristo, past the birthplace of Pablo Picasso in the Plaza de la Merced, and into the historic district. The Faculty of Philosophy and Liberal Arts was located in an ancient, three-story building on a narrow street near the cathedral. An open corridor on each level of classrooms overlooked a European-style courtyard with a fountain in the center. It felt like I had stepped back in time and been transported to a magical place with constant sunshine.

My classmates for the international program were nineteen strikingly diverse individuals from Germany, France, Japan, the United States, Egypt, and The Netherlands. I recall that they wore an assortment of jeans, flowing shirts, and brightly colored scarves and were altogether different from anyone I had encountered before, even on the farm.

The classes were in Spanish and comprised language, literature, history, and art history. I purchased the required books and enjoyed the lessons, especially literature, taught by Doña Maria del Pilar Palomo, an esteemed academic who had written several books and whose love of literature was palpable. I slipped seamlessly into a routine, joining my fellow students after class in *La Buena Sombra*, a bustling student bodega.

The political situation in Spain was still tumultuous. General Franco had died, and there was hope for free and fair elections for the first time in 40 years. We encountered regular street demonstrations and attended musical events promoting freedom of speech. One day, I was in the Buena Sombra with friends when gunshots were heard outside. The security partition was pulled down, and no one could leave for half an hour. There was certainly no lack of excitement in this historic city.

# CHAPTER 26

# Traveling Around Andalucia

Aside from my European friends, I enjoyed the company of my American classmates—Antoinette, a vibrant, third-generation Italian American, and Eduardo, a Puerto Rican who spent his childhood on various U.S. army bases as his family moved from one place to another. I admit my previous idea of Americans was that they were primarily white, loud, and wore shorts. I'm not sure where I acquired this stereotype—suffice it to say that my focus had always been on Europe. Antoinette and Eduardo, however, were olive-skinned, knowledgeable about the arts and music, kind, self-deprecating, and fun to be with. I liked them immediately, and Antoinette is still a good friend today.

One weekend, I planned a day trip with Eduardo, and we agreed to meet on a corner in town. Eduardo was soft-spoken and good-looking, and I had a crush on him during my first few weeks in Spain. Arriving a little late at our meeting spot, I noticed he was surrounded by a group of local men who appeared to be taunting him. Eduardo looked distinctly uncomfortable: his straight-leg indigo jeans were tucked into new-looking leather cowboy boots, his stylish shirt fit perfectly, and the expression on his face screamed *HELP!*

A couple of things happened simultaneously—first, it dawned on me that Eduardo was gay. At the same time, without hesitating, I pushed through the semicircle of guys, greeted Eduardo warmly with a kiss on the cheek, grabbed his arm, and led him away from the assembled locals, who were now looking confused. Eduardo's expression of relief was endearing. I don't remember where we went that day, but I know he was a good friend of Antoinette's and mine and that we often talked and spent time together during our stay in Spain.

Málaga is surrounded by dry, mountainous countryside, home to many *pueblos blancos*, white villages tucked into the mountain landscape. One of my happiest memories is walking along dusty country roads flanked by olive groves and turning a bend to see a tiny village in the distance. Then, on arrival at the village, exploring the narrow winding streets, ducking into a café or bar for shade and refreshment, and conversing with the locals.

I sometimes traveled alone but mostly took a bus with friends or found a ride with them. A recurrent theme is that I have always felt something transcendent when walking and exploring, and this feeling was heightened in Spain. The villages closest to the Costa Del Sol, such as Mijas and Benalmadena, were predictably touristy and could be visited in a day. However, farther inland, exquisitely remote villages lay waiting to be explored.

The ancient cities of Seville, Cordoba, and Granada are farther inland still. We visited each of these on weekends, and I remember feeling entranced by the intricate mosaics, delicate arches, and fountains of the Alhambra Palace in Granada. Only a few tourists were there on the day we visited—maybe because it was early morning—contributing to our ability to soak up the peaceful environment.

It wasn't long before it became apparent that my funds were running out—did I mention that I didn't always think things through in my late teens and early twenties? Pedro stepped in and kindly arranged for me to teach English conversation to him and two of his teacher friends three evenings a week. We agreed on an amount, which I assumed would be paid by each of them, but, of course, they meant the total sum, which was logical but a disappointment at the time. Still, I enjoyed conversing with the three of them in their varying degrees of tortured English and scraped by financially until Christmas.

# CHAPTER 27

# The Crazy Cottage

By December, I was starting to miss home and decided to return for Christmas. I was happy to see my parents and friends again, although I felt strangely suspended between my home and traveling lives. Naturally, my friends asked, "How was Spain?" I found it hard to respond, as if they were asking *How is life on Mars?* I was grateful they were still there for me, though, despite my disappearing regularly.

Back in Málaga, in the New Year, I found a part-time job teaching English to three elementary school-age sisters in their home. This helped boost my finances, and their family, the Garcías, welcomed me, often inviting me to stay for a dinner of Spanish omelets in their compact, high-rise flat. One evening, while teaching in their living room, the table started shaking. Thinking the girls were playing a trick on me, I looked under the table, but then the cabinets began to shake, too, and I realized it was an earthquake. The tremor subsided almost as soon as I understood what was happening, so there was no time to be afraid or to do anything. Another first!

I said goodbye to Doña Concha and Delores early in the New Year. Several of my classmates lived in a beach cottage in the fishing village of Pedregalejo, a few miles east of Málaga. The rent was cheap, and it sounded enticing. Pedregalejo consisted of two or three narrow dirt roads with low-slung houses, fishing shacks, and a general store—all running parallel to a stony beach.

In addition to my classmates, a couple of Spaniards involved in the local political scene also lived there. Antoinette called it the crazy cottage, an apt description. Random travelers often visited, and it reminded me of James Michener's *The Drifters* about Torremolinos in the 1960s. The linoleum floor was invariably sticky from a mixture of dirt and wine, and the furniture was falling apart.

*The crazy cottage*

Despite the downsides, I enjoyed living close to fishing families, students, activists, and musicians and felt part of the community as I walked along the dirt track to the store. With no Dolores to cook, my go-to meal of necessity was baked bean omelets—the name sounds better in Spanish: *tortillas de alubias con salsa de tomate*—sloppy but satisfying.

In the evenings, we sang and played guitars in the living room. I provided the English vocals to popular songs such as "Something" by George Harrison, with a skilled guitarist playing the accompaniment and intricate riffs.

Whenever I needed some peace, the Mediterranean was ten meters away. Watching gentle waves lap against rocks in the cool night air, I contemplated life and the universe from that spot. I believe I saw a UFO there, too—a bright light in the sky that hovered over the coast, swooped away in an arc, and disappeared. No, I wasn't on drugs—I never have taken any illegal substances. I will admit, though, that I embraced other aspects of 1970s drifter life during my time there.

A rustic beach bar called *Miguelito El Cariñoso* stood across the track from the ramshackle cottage. The owner, Miguel, in his forties, was always kind to us, his multi-national student neighbors. His *boquerones* (fresh anchovies), grilled on a stick, were the best!

Returning to the present, in 2022—45 years later—my husband, Dale, and I visited the current Miguelito El Cariñoso restaurant, still housed in the same spot but remodeled and updated. We introduced ourselves to Miguel's wife and family, who told us that Miguel had passed away in 2007. We lunched on boquerones and gazpacho soup and were welcomed like old friends. The streets in Pedregalejo hadn't changed much, but now it's a popular spot for malagueños and tourists to visit, with its "authentic fishing village" vibe. I looked over to where the cottage had been but couldn't place it in the row of renovated beach homes, although Miguel's widow assured me it was still there.

# CHAPTER 28

# Morocco

A few miles across the Mediterranean, Morocco seemed a logical place to visit for Spring break. An English friend, Denise, and I took a ferry to the port town of Ceuta and a bus inland. Our fellow bus passengers included a woman holding a cage containing several hens and a man with a large tumor sticking out of his turban. We stayed at a rowdy hostel in Meknes and didn't get much sleep that first night.

Getting used to Morocco's noise, heat, and bustle took a while. On the second day, we continued to the town of Fez, where a boy offered to show us the medina, a vast, bustling market located within a maze of narrow streets. We wandered along narrow alleys between ancient buildings, passing tiny stores, their wares displayed outside. The scent of herbs and spices, leather goods, and sweet treats mingled in an exotic blend, accentuated by the colorful visuals of indigenous Berber crafts. I can't remember if we paid the boy to enter the medina, but he charmingly told us we'd need to pay him to show us the way out, and we complied. Denise and I then spent the afternoon drinking mint tea at an outdoor café, overlooking the ornate tower of a minaret, and conversing with a local couple in French while attempting to learn a few words of Arabic.

The next day's destination was Oujda. I recall a large town square flanked by vendors, where we purchased nuts and dates for a snack with our dwindling resources. The banging of a drum in the center of the square, accompanied by a man screaming, caught our attention. Moving closer, we realized he was having teeth removed, seemingly without anesthesia—at least, that's how I remember it.

That evening, Denise and I accepted a ride from a local, who told us he was heading to the ferry port for our return trip to Spain. All seemed to be going well until our vehicle was intercepted by a police car, siren blaring, and our driver was arrested. There was much yelling in Arabic, so we weren't sure what was going on, but it occurred to me later that we were only a couple of miles from the Algerian border. Were we about to be abducted? The policeman then turned his attention to us, scolding us for accepting the ride, before arranging our overnight stay at a nearby guest house. That night, another man knocked on our door several times, requesting to speak with us in polite French with an Arabic accent. We ignored him and eventually went to sleep. Overall, we were fortunate to come out of this adventure unscathed. I'm grateful to the policeman and whoever else was watching over us.

In the morning, we caught a bus to the port town of Melilla. Relaxing on the beach, we ate *churros*—inexpensive and comfortingly familiar lengths of sugary fried dough, popular in Spain—before catching the ferry back.

# CHAPTER 29

# Cottage Life and My Parents Visit

Back in Málaga, excitement about the upcoming elections was reaching fever pitch as, for the first time in forty years, various political parties would participate in the electoral process rather than being repressed under Franco's regime. There were chants of "*El pueblo unido, jamás sera vencido*" (The people united will never be divided), and "*Legalización de todos los partidos*" (Legalization of every single party). History was being made! Works by poets such as Antonio Machado, who had died in exile, and others who had perished during the Spanish Civil War were put to music and sung by contemporary artists. These songs, among other popular English and American anthems of the era, were played in the cottage during the evenings, and I learned some of them on my guitar.

We often participated in whatever was happening locally. I recall a rally featuring a formerly exiled political leader, when we were swept into the football stadium by the surging crowd—even the football pitch was packed to bursting. I don't recall anything about the speech, but I was certainly grateful we got out without being trampled, as there was no visible security.

On a different day, a friend and I learned that a Málaga beach close to the port was about to open for topless sunbathing, so we went along to check it out. On arrival, we saw a group of local guys congregating expectantly along the high port wall. They reminded me of the gargoyles of Notre Dame, and I realized that this was not going to work. Málaga was different from the nearby resort town of Marbella, where a European-style topless beach would be considered normal. As it happened, no one disrobed, and the guys dispersed. I don't remember if my friend stayed or left.

I mention this day, though, because I spent the afternoon on the beach, in a tee shirt and shorts, reading *Loose Change* by journalist Sara Davidson. The book details Davidson's life in Berkeley, California, in the 1960s, not so different from our life in 1970s Spain. It occurred to me that I was tired of translating and wanted to write. After finishing the book, I brushed off the sand, picked up my tote bag, and headed back up the port steps, contemplating how to fit writing lessons into my life.

The only other event of note during my cottage days was that my parents visited from England. They traveled via train, ship, and two more trains, a journey of some 1,300 miles, and looked alarmingly exhausted when I met them at Málaga train station. They stayed at a hotel overlooking the promenade, where I visited daily to show them around.

This was the only time my parents ever saw me while I was traveling, and it was the most run-down living situation I had ever experienced. The cottage was falling apart, and the linoleum floor refused to come clean despite my best efforts. Naturally, my parents assumed, from then on, that wherever I lived abroad was similar to the cottage. They were nice about it, though, and I introduced them to all my friends there. We took a day trip, climbing winding mountain roads by bus to the picturesque town of Ronda. Another day, I took them to see the ancient caves in Nerja. My parents enjoyed their Spanish holiday, and Mum even made a valiant attempt to learn Spanish from then on.

# CHAPTER 30

# A Peaceful Apartment

I was starting to tire of the cottage. The overly relaxed attitude of some of my roommates and their unwillingness to pitch in with cleaning or organizing, along with one individual's annoying habit of starting every other sentence with "When the revolution comes . . ." made me realize I was ready for a change.

Coincidentally, Antoinette had secured a small apartment overlooking the Mediterranean for the rest of the summer and asked if I'd like to move in with her. The owner, a retired American firefighter, was going away and needed someone to water the garlic plants on his balcony.

My last six weeks in Málaga were spent with Antoinette in the compact, clean apartment. I'm tempted to say everything went smoothly, but there was one more incident. We took a trip to Nerja, the coastal town to the east I had visited with my parents. Antoinette and I wandered around town, stopping for lunch and taking in the view from the *Balcón de Europa*, a semi-circular observation balcony overlooking the sea. At the end of the afternoon, as we left the town square, three young workers in a cargo van offered us a ride back to Málaga. In my defense, I recall pausing to contemplate if it was a good idea: there were two of us; I knew the coast road well; they looked harmless—what could possibly go wrong? Antoinette and I climbed into the back section of the van, with the three men in the front, setting off along the coast road.

A sudden jolt knocked us sideways as the van veered off the main road to the right and onto a dirt track toward the mountains. Not wasting any time, I scrambled over to the van's side door, heaved it open, and told Antoinette to jump—which she did. The van swerved as the driver looked over his shoulder, and then I jumped too, landing on the dusty verge a few yards farther along than Antoinette. I was fired up and angry—partly at myself because I had endangered my friend by accepting the ride and making her jump. Plus, I was fed up with not being able to trust people. I ran at the young men, kicking, shouting, and swinging my bag at them, and they retreated into their van and drove off. Antoinette seemed okay, although I'm sure she must have been shaken and had some bruises. I have no recollection of how we got home.

Aside from that one hiccough, our last few weeks in Spain were relaxing and enjoyable. We read books on our balcony, visited friends along the coast, and went dancing with Eduardo in Torremolinos and Benalmadena. Harvesting our host's garlic plants was not as successful as planned, as they had mostly shriveled, but aside from that, everything went well.

As university classes ended and the summer heat increased, my classmates started returning to their respective countries, and it was time for me to leave, too. Here's a song I wrote that is loosely based on life in Spain and the cottage:

## The Drifters

All over the world, the children cried
We don't want to grow up like you
This life is okay if you're satisfied
But we want to find something new
Your duty ends here, Dad, so it's thanks and goodbye
It's time for me to defect
You've done nothing wrong, Mum, so please don't cry
We need someone sound to reject

So, the multi-national, jean-clad drifters, we
Left home in search of the sun
We lived in a house where an olive tree
Reached out to welcome everyone
We shared our possessions and suntanned our bodies
Swam in the sea, read Jung, Jong, and Yates
We talked about freedom, who we were, who God is
And lived on checks from Japan and the States

Those misty emotional hours flowed into summer
With the help of music and wine
Until that fateful day when the landlord came
And said, "Get out now, kids; it's tourist time"
So, goodbye to the pueblo as the painters rolled in
Splashing whitewash on our sacred olive tree
It was fun while it lasted (but did I really fit in?)
So, it was back home to the U.K. for me

Fellow drifters, if you're listening: Hey now, don't get mad
If Don Quijote was crazy, then so were we
And sometimes, I think the real world is twice as bad
And I miss your company
Perhaps one day, we'll learn to reach out and give
Like that fated olive tree in the sand
But until then, please forgive us if we need to run and live
In some far-off, flaky, never-never-land

I was scrambling to pay my way in Spain, but I recall a classmate wandering around the cottage, stressed that his funds hadn't arrived from Japan. Also, it's true that everyone had to leave the cottage when the tourist season started, but I had already moved in with Antoinette by then.

My year in Malaga was one I'll never forget, and I'm glad I decided to leave my translating job and try something new.

# CHAPTER 31

# Whisky Exports
# and Visiting Antoinette

Back in England, I found a job working for a whisky export company, commuting by train to London each day. The scotch was sold in bottles whose shape and labels resembled famous brands, but the quality of the whisky inside may have been less than top shelf. My boss covered Europe and Latin America, and I typed letters in French and Spanish and helped him receive clients from overseas. I made the most of his frequent sales trips abroad, taking extended lunch breaks and happily exploring London's West End.

Not forgetting my determination on the beach in Málaga, I completed two correspondence courses with the London School of Journalism, submitting assignments by mail and eagerly awaiting the return envelopes with feedback from my professor. I read numerous magazines, newspapers, and books on my daily commute, familiarizing myself with contemporary writers such as Anna Raeburn and Jilly Cooper and their commentaries on London life and current events. I was also becoming more interested in New York and the United States, inspired by letters and books Antoinette sent me. I think I saw the film *Annie Hall* three times.

Inevitably, as summer rolled around the following year, I was itching to travel again. Antoinette invited me to visit her in Harrisburg, Pennsylvania, and I wasted no time giving in my notice at the whisky company. We planned a road trip around the northeastern United States, visiting various members of Antoinette's sizeable Italian-American family and her friends. I didn't own a car and was still riding my Honda 70, so I left my driver's license in England. Poor Antoinette was left to drive the entire trip—I still feel bad about that.

Landing at JFK Airport, I surveyed the packed arrivals hall to see Antoinette jumping up and down and waving. Antoinette is not tall, so the jumping helped. We set off toward her friend's house on Long Island, getting lost and asking directions at a gas station in the curiously named town of Hicksville. Finally locating our destination in Rockville Center, Brian greeted us warmly, taking us sightseeing in New York City during our weekend stay. We took photos from the top of the World Trade Center and walked around Greenwich Village, Chelsea, and Washington Square—places I was familiar with from songs by Joan Baez and Joni Mitchell. On Sunday morning, we ate bagels with cream cheese and read the New York Times in Brian's comfortable suburban home before visiting another of Antoinette's friends, who lived in a commune on the tip of Long Island. Everything was new and exciting while, at the same time, strangely familiar.

Back on the road, we crossed the Verrazano Bridge overlooking New York Harbor. We then continued through New Jersey to rural Pennsylvania, where Antoinette's sister, Rosemary, lived with her husband and daughters. They kindly welcomed me in their Camp Hill home, and I recall snacking on pretzels, drinking chilled bottles of beer, and reading picture books to Antoinette's young nieces, trying out my American accent.

It was a whirlwind trip, so I apologize if this reads like a travelogue. We spent a couple of days visiting local Pennsylvania sites: a day trip to the Hershey chocolate factory and a visit to the Gettysburg battlefield site. The latter involved a presentation where a hokey, mechanical Abraham Lincoln rose through the floor to deliver the President's famous Gettysburg Address. We stopped at a nearby Amish town, where locals in old-fashioned clothing drove horse-drawn buggies, and we dined at a nearby all-you-can-eat Smorgasbord. The all-you-can-eat concept was new to me, and American diner portion sizes still astound me today.

Next was a visit to one of Antoinette's brothers in Maryland, where he kindly took us out on the expansive Chesapeake Bay in his sailboat. We then spent a family weekend in a country cabin in the peaceful Pocono mountains of Pennsylvania. I loved spending time with this sweet family and enjoyed every minute.

The grand tour of our road trip was when we all drove, in two cars, to visit another of Antoinette and Rosemary's brothers in Chicago. This 650-mile drive helped me grasp the immensity of the United States (as a child, the 20 miles to Brighton seemed like a long distance). Breaking up our journey with an overnight motel stay in Angola, Indiana, we pulled into a local bar-and-grill for dinner. No sooner had our food arrived than we noticed locals at the bar directing stares and comments at Antoinette's brother-in-law, accompanied as he was by three women. We finished our meals quickly and were relieved to leave that little slice of Americana behind.

Antoinette's oldest brother and his wife were professors at the University of Chicago, and we stayed at their home in a historic neighborhood. We visited the Science Museum and an Art Museum, where I was astonished at how much European art must have found its way to the United States. We also surveyed the city from the top of the Hancock Building and took a boat trip along the river.

After Chicago, Antoinette and I continued to Canada while the others returned to Pennsylvania. In his seventies, my dad's brother, Jack, lived in Ontario with his extended family. The drive from Chicago was long, and I made the mistake of thinking Uncle Jack lived in Toronto, whereas Peterborough lies one and a half hours to the other side. Poor Antoinette was exhausted from driving the whole way, and again, I felt mortified that I wasn't helping out.

*With Antoinette in Canada*

Unlike my dad in every way, Jack, despite his advancing years, was energetic, outgoing, and a fan of country music. He and his family made us feel at home, with a barbecue and swimming in their backyard pool and also took us go-karting.

On our return trip across the border, we stopped in Syracuse, NY, to visit another of Antoinette's friends. I was surprised by the peaceful pine forests and mountains of upstate New York, not realizing I would one day live in the Hudson Valley.

The last stop was back to Brian's in Rockville Center for a few days. Antoinette was job-hunting and embarked on her search in New York City while I was free to explore, meeting up with her between interviews. I accompanied her to one agency, however, resulting in a future magazine article called "Job Hunting, New York Style."

On my first solo subway ride, I decided to return to Greenwich Village, which I knew was around Sixth Street. Riding a train that was supposed to be heading there, I was alarmed to see Manhattan receding in the distance as we rattled across a bridge into Brooklyn. At Sixth Street in Brooklyn, I got off and found my way back to the Village, as I recall. The vibrancy of Washington Square was enchanting, with its multi-ethnic, youthful spirit and people mingling around the fountain in the summer sun.

Brian kindly prepared dinner for us on our last night at his home. It had been an incredible trip, thanks to Antoinette's valiant driving and her family's overwhelming kindness. I felt sad about leaving my good friend and also had a slight feeling of nostalgia that, somehow, I was meant to live in the United States or Canada. I put the thought behind me and enjoyed the evening, planning to return someday.

# CHAPTER 32

# Returning to France and Spain

After several months of temping in London, I tried replicating my Spanish experience in the South of France. Mum asked why I needed to go away again. Honestly, I wasn't sure—it must have been hard for her. Nonetheless, I had saved some money and took a plane to Aix-en-Provence, a student town.

But it wasn't the same—partly because I hadn't enrolled in a program or booked anywhere to live in advance. I rented a room near the university campus but wasn't connected to anything happening there. I sat at outdoor cafés on beautiful boulevards with palm trees, but no one spoke to me. I made feeble attempts to find a job with no luck. A strange sense of loneliness started creeping in for the first time, and I wasn't sure what to do with it. I took a bus trip to the historic town of Avignon and tried to take in the sights, but generally, things weren't going well.

Following a footpath that cut across campus back to my lodgings one evening, I found the campus gate locked—it was a national holiday. Turning to retrace my steps, I encountered two young men in their twenties, one wielding a knife. It was eerily quiet as they backed me up against the fence—I'm not a screamer by nature. One of the guys pressed the knife blade against my neck with one hand and felt my breast with the other. I focused on his buddy, speaking calmly and carefully in French to avoid disturbing the knife.

"*Ça ne va pas, non?* Are you crazy? What if someone treated your sister this way?" Ignoring knife-guy, I maintained eye contact and continued speaking with his buddy, who eventually responded with the French equivalent of "Come on, man, that's enough. Let's go."

The perpetrator lowered the knife and stepped back, and I pushed past them, retracing my steps to the road and walking around the campus exterior. Shaken and trembling, I decided I'd had enough of Aix. On arriving at my room, I packed my stuff, paid the landlady, and headed to the train station—and Spain.

One problem with emotional states is that they tend to remain the same even with a change of location. I disembarked in Barcelona on a whim, with the idea of seeing the sights but, failing to shake the feeling of loneliness, returned to the station after a few hours, purchasing a ticket to Málaga.

The overnight train was calm when I boarded, and I located a compartment with a woman, probably in her forties, seated in the opposite corner. We greeted each other briefly before I settled back in my seat and fell asleep, exhausted.

"Excuse me, Señorita." A voice seemed to be addressing me, but I ignored it, hoping I was dreaming,

"*Señorita!*" The tone was apologetic but insistent, and I reluctantly opened my eyes to see a sailor in uniform.

"*Ah, Señorita, Buenas noches. Es que . . .*" Having woken me up, he seemed hesitant to speak.

"*Buenas noches. Que pasa?*" I wanted him to say whatever it was so I could go back to sleep.

"It's that . . . my commanding officer and the Señora here would like to . . . have relations, so please, can you leave the compartment to give them some privacy?"

My Spanish comprehension left no room for misunderstanding, but I still couldn't believe what I was hearing. I glanced at the woman, who gazed back at us, expressionless. I then made the sailor repeat his request one more time, a little more explicitly, to ensure I'd got it right. Feeling betrayed and exasperated, I pulled my backpack off the rack and headed into the corridor. In retrospect, I could have said no, and I also should have checked with the woman to make sure she knew what was going on, but I didn't think of either of those things at the time.

There were no vacant seats on the train, packed as it now was with Spanish sailors, even lining the corridor. *What are they all doing on this train? Aren't they supposed to travel by ship?* I was beyond frustrated. Picking my way around the sailors to the end of the corridor, I found several of them seated or sprawled in the extra space, leaning against the wall. In contrast to my previous experience on the French train, these men seemed more tired than drunk, but I didn't want to take any chances.

Noticing a tiny space next to a young sailor, I squeezed onto the floor beside him and started chatting, getting just a little cozy and adopting him for the remainder of the trip. After a while, Juan Carlos put his arm around me protectively, and I fell asleep undisturbed—despite the creaking train—clutching my backpack to my chest.

Arriving in Málaga, Juan Carlos accompanied me out of the station. He looked even younger in the early morning sunshine—as opposed to my mature 23 years (I'm joking). We started walking east toward town, and he tentatively suggested getting a hotel room together. "*Si te parece bien*" (if you'd like)—he was a polite young man. I couldn't fault him for trying, as I had essentially used him as a prop to survive the journey. I smiled warmly, said I needed to be elsewhere, and set off with a renewed lightness to my step. Wondering where the sadness had gone as I skirted the Paseo del Parque on my way to the Garcías home, I realized I had navigated the past sixteen hours and come out unscathed. I was, somehow, no longer concerned about being victimized and felt confident I could deal with whatever life threw at me. As it happens, there have been no more assaults to date.

The Garcías greeted me warmly, their young girls excited to see me again. The family somehow knew of an empty one-bedroom flat in town and made it seem like I was doing them a favor by staying there rent-free. I spent a few days tracking down old friends, my former English students, and one classmate who had remained in Málaga and now had a Spanish husband and baby. I enjoyed playing with the baby and chatting with my friend, contemplating what my life might have been like if I had stayed. Interesting as it was to imagine this path, I decided I was happy to have moved on.

My friend, Sasha, from Pinetree Farm, whom I had previously visited in Brussels, was now living with her family in a hacienda-style home in the Andalucian countryside and invited me to visit. We swam in her pool, rode horses, listened to Supertramp and Cat Stevens albums, and generally lounged around. I recall riding through an orange grove, grabbing an orange, peeling and eating it—still on horseback. The landscape was hilly, dotted with olive and orange groves, typical of the area. Another memory is of scrambling, on foot, up a rocky hill near her home and almost putting my hand on a giant snake sunbathing there.

Looking back, I'm amazed at how I nonchalantly assumed staying with friends was no big deal. I always felt welcomed, which is humbling, and I genuinely appreciate those who took me in. I continue to be astonished by the kindness of others.

My last few weeks in Spain were spent between Sasha's place in the countryside and the flat in Malaga. Lucy visited from England, and we were invited to the Garcías seaside condo, farther along the coast, for a week. When not relaxing on the beach, we toured my favorite spots around Málaga and the Costa del Sol. I'm forever grateful to the García family for their friendship and hospitality. That period in Spain was liberating because I felt able to live in the moment, unconcerned about the future, knowing I would eventually return to England.

# CHAPTER 33

# Moving to London

It was time to move out of my parents' flat in Crowborough and live in London. I found a fourth-floor walk-up in Earls Court, a multi-racial neighborhood in Southwest London, close to the more upmarket areas of Kensington and Chelsea, without being as expensive. My roommates were two upper-class 19-year-old guys and two girls around my age. My room was tiny. Not only did it have a sloping ceiling—relatively standard for an attic flat—but the floor sloped as well. I loved my room and the vibrant neighborhood.

It didn't take long to get used to London life. My roommates were sweet, and we socialized occasionally, although we weren't that close. I joined an organization called "London Link Up," with various activities you can participate in or create yourself. I played squash, went swimming at a college pool, and started an acoustic guitar club called "Strum and Wail." I went on a few dates with fellow Link-Up lads but was still more interested in making friends than settling down. One friend, Carol, invited me to Birmingham to visit her college friends for a weekend. Relaxing in her friends' messy communal flat reminded me of my cottage days in Spain. We had an enjoyable time, but it was good to note that I was no longer interested in that lifestyle.

Temporary jobs were easy to find, and I started with those. However, a newspaper ad caught my attention one Friday evening on the Crowborough-bound train to see my parents. It read, *Wanted, bi-lingual Spanish/English personal assistant for villa sales in Spain.* Wasting no time, I jumped off at the next station, calling the company from a platform payphone and securing an interview for the upcoming Monday afternoon.

The company was run by Eddie, a middle-aged Yorkshireman, out of a messy, cramped office on the outskirts of London. I was offered the job and joined three other young women preparing for the following weekend's trip to the Costa Del Sol, near Málaga. Eddie warned me I'd have only one free weekend per month, but I didn't care, as it sounded too interesting to pass up.

The job entailed escorting a group of a dozen or so prospective clients each weekend, staying at a hotel in the tourist resort of Torremolinos. It was billed as a free weekend for prospective buyers and attracted some folk who were less than serious, so there was a determined sales pitch. Our outgoing plane that weekend was delayed due to fog at London's Gatwick Airport, so we checked into our Torremolinos hotel late Friday night. I was ready for bed but was informed we were going out, so I climbed into a van with the rest of the crew.

The outing, I learned, was to visit a co-worker who had just undergone an abortion, having gotten pregnant on the job. The group crammed into her hotel room, wishing her well, eating cake on her bed, and drinking champagne. This was decidedly weird, but I had the upcoming weekend to worry about, so I tried to put it out of my mind.

Saturday was a coach bus tour along the Costa del Sol, from Torremolinos to Marbella, visiting a series of newly constructed flats—so far, so good. On Sunday, however, my co-workers and I were each expected to drive a smaller group back to the flats they liked most. I still hadn't driven a car since passing my test five years previously.

Sunday morning dawned, and I gathered my group of three unsuspecting Brits from the hotel lobby, heading west along the coast road in the rented car. Aside from my less-than-stellar driving skills, the next challenge was finding the addresses and locating the correct keys from the bunch I'd been given to access the properties. The Costa del Sol in the seventies was a mass of hastily assembled construction projects—"villas," according to the brochures—and they mostly looked alike. I made a couple of wrong turns, and it took a while to get some of the keys to work despite my helpful compatriots volunteering to "have a go." It was a stressful day, but we made it back to Torremolinos in one piece, having viewed most of the relevant properties.

Our guests were free to relax and enjoy the resort for the remainder of Sunday. Eddie informed me that a man in my group was interested in purchasing a flat and that I should stick with him throughout the evening and encourage him to buy. At this point, it occurred to me that this was possibly how one of my co-workers became pregnant. I spent a pleasant evening with the prospective client, chatting over sangria at an outdoor café—and then we said goodnight.

The next morning, awaiting our return flight at Málaga airport, Eddie approached me in good spirits. My client had put down a deposit on a flat.

"Well done, lass! Not many girls make a sale on their first weekend." He presented me with a wad of cash right there in the departure lounge.

Back in London, I mulled over the experience. I felt out of my depth but could have made a lot of money—one co-worker drove a Ferrari. But who was I kidding? I've never been into material things, and the operation looked somewhat shady. I called Eddie that afternoon to say I wasn't returning and chalked it up to experience.

CHAPTER 34

# Writing and The Spanish Embassy

was still temping, but my focus was on writing short, humorous articles and trying to get them published. One day, I left my temp office in the pouring rain for a pub lunch appointment with the editor of *Metro*, a new weekly London publication handed out at train stations. Ducking into the pub, I sat down with the young woman, who said she liked the piece I had submitted and asked if I was aiming for *Cosmo*.

Invited back to the *Metro* office later that week, I was told they'd publish the piece—a light-hearted look at commuter travel. They also offered to consider anything else I'd like to submit and handed me a bottle of Champagne—bizarre but true. I was excited and started dreaming about other stories I could write for them.

Another magazine, *Jobs Weekly*, subsequently published three more pieces: one about working as a trilingual secretary, one about job-hunting with Antoinette in New York, and a third about the San Francisco job market. But I'm getting ahead of myself.

My last full-time job in London was at the Spanish Embassy as assistant to the commercial attaché. The embassy was in Belgravia, but the commercial office was in trendy Knightsbridge, behind Harrods department store, a few tube stops from my flat. I discovered that Harrods has an excellent bakery, and I often stopped there for bread on my way home from work.

Everyone working in the commercial department was Spanish, aside from one older British woman who was fluent. Speaking and writing Spanish constantly was stimulating, and we went to occasional dinner parties at the Embassy itself. My job was assisting my young boss and logging in the various daily fruit imports—not exactly thrilling, but I liked the relaxed environment and stayed there for almost a year.

A few weeks before my 24th birthday, I was walking on the village green in Crowborough when I saw a clear image of a screen hovering above eye level to the right. Most of the screen was of my current life—always on the go, with friends and brief relationships, and it was pretty good. However, one section of the screen was more vivid, highly defined, and included children and grandchildren. In my daydream, I sensed that I wanted to move from my present reality to the deeper one—then it vanished.

On turning 24, I sat on my bed in Earls Court and contemplated, in my journal, whether I wanted to settle down and have children eventually. I concluded that I did and that 28 would be a good age to get serious about that.

One evening, arriving back in Earls Court after work, I found a flyer in my letterbox advertising a yoga class in Knightsbridge. Intrigued, I signed up for the course and headed there the following week. In addition to teaching the various *asanas*, our instructor explained other health and spiritual aspects of yoga, which I found fascinating. My classmates were diverse and engaging, and we sometimes got together in a Knightsbridge pub after class. I practiced yoga in my flat, placing the mat on my sloping bedroom floor and incorporating meditation and healthy eating habits into my routine. I was sad when the course ended after eight weeks, but I continued my yoga practice. Newly curious about Eastern philosophy and spirituality, I visited the Kensington Library to borrow books and study.

I returned to Crowborough every few weekends to check on my parents and visit friends. Mum had been experiencing back pain and looked tired, and Dad seemed less stable when walking. I helped with housework when I was home, but I knew I wouldn't be living in Crowborough again for the long term. Did I feel conflicted about this? Yes, absolutely. My parents always supported my lifestyle, but I still wish I'd better cared for them in their older years.

# CHAPTER 35

# Return to the United States

Sitting in an Earl's Court launderette, watching my sudsy clothes rotate, I felt the familiar longing to travel again. A Swiss friend from my time in Málaga was planning to visit her boyfriend in San Diego and asked if I'd like to go to San Francisco with her. The timing was right, as I had wondered where I could learn more about yoga and spirituality and hopefully find a synthesis of Eastern and Western thought. Meanwhile, another friend had suggested a trip to India, but remembering my discomforting Moroccan experience, I chose California.

The plan was to spend a few days in San Francisco and then travel down the coast to San Diego. I didn't know what I'd do once my friend joined her boyfriend, but I had a vague idea of perhaps finding a community in the Los Angeles area. I had been contemplating a return to the United States, and this was my chance.

I contacted Jobs Weekly and received a commission to write an article about the San Francisco job market. Also, a few weeks previously, I attended a press conference given by singer and activist Joan Baez after her concert in North London. Baez had spoken of a human rights organization she founded with her mother, based in Menlo Park, near San

Francisco. Perhaps I could volunteer there. I wrote to Joan Baez and received a kind response from her mother, as I recall, but I didn't visit.

Flying over the Rocky Mountains with my Swiss friend, it occurred to me that I needed to be focused. I determined to neither drink alcohol nor eat the delicious salty pretzels I'd discovered on my previous trip to the U.S. Sitting back in my seat, I relaxed, waiting for my new adventure to begin, not suspecting that I was about to land in a country I'd eventually call home.

CHAPTER 36

# Looking Back

It seems fitting to end this memoir here. I think enough happened for one book, don't you? Looking back 44 years later, I'm glad I followed that invisible thread of intuition that kept me traveling and seeking new experiences. I feel fortunate that my next step always seemed to appear when needed. There were decisions to make and hurdles to overcome, but my path mostly flowed, for which I'm overwhelmingly grateful. Some of my friends have continued to live close to home (making them easier to track down), while others are still roaming the planet. Each person's path is unique. As I said at the beginning, everyone has a story to tell.

I found a community in San Francisco and stayed in the Bay Area for almost two years, volunteering with a small group of international travelers in a minority neighborhood south of the city. The vibe in our household was friendly, coed monasticism, and it was refreshing to be around guys who weren't trying to hit on me. Maybe I needed that, along with the structure and continuity the Unification community provided. These days, I'm no longer closely affiliated with any group, preferring to look inside myself for guidance, but I still have good friends from my time there.

The next few years took me to several countries, including Wales, to visit Lucy, who proudly showed me around her sheep farm in the Welsh mountains. And yes, there were many crazy adventures and learning experiences along the way—some things never change—but those details are for another day.

I met my husband, Dale, in 1987, and we settled in Ossining, on the Hudson River, north of New York City, where we still live. Dale is a quiet, thoughtful American from Pittsburgh. He plays the guitar, has a retirement business fixing clarinets, and is my life partner, my love. Raising our three children, now adults, has been the privilege of a lifetime. I'm genuinely in awe of these kind-hearted, intelligent, funny individuals, and I look forward to meeting future additions to our family.

Work-wise, I found something I enjoyed and could stay at for more than a few months. Or maybe I matured—now, there's a thought! Using my languages, I traveled with an international foundation based in New York City for three years. Later, I worked at an innovative art company that offered flexibility so that I could focus on our family.

I continued to visit Mum and Dad in England until they passed in 1989 and 1998, respectively. Mum died when I became pregnant with our first child, Elana. I returned to England for her funeral service in December of 1989, and Dale flew over to join Dad and me for Christmas. It was a sad time, and I remember consoling myself with several delicious sandwiches Paul's wife, Pauline, had kindly prepared. Back in New York, I couldn't fit into my clothes, and a pregnancy test confirmed why.

Despite various ailments, Mum always maintained her cheerful disposition and salty humor. Just as I feel close to my Nan, I sense Mum is just a smile and a breath away. She seems closer now than when she lived across the Atlantic Ocean.

Dad met all three of his grandchildren as we visited England several times—the last being when James, our youngest, was a toddler. Having finally become comfortable driving, I rented a car with a kiddie car seat for our visits. Dad was ecstatic about "going for a spin" on summer evenings, stopping at his favorite pubs for a pint.

On one visit to Pinetree Farm, Bunty and Tommy hosted a barbecue for us in their garden—complete with a marquee tent—inviting many friends I hadn't seen for years. Their kindness completely blew me away, and after it was over, our elder son, Kent, asked,

"How are we related to all these people, again?"

"We're not, Kent. They're just really, really good friends."

I will always be grateful to Bunty and Tommy Douglas of Pinetree Farm and their daughter, Susie, for including me in their international family.

Dad continued to watch birds and study Spanish and mathematics throughout his life. Outliving Mum by nine years, he moved from Craigmore Hall to a lovely country rest home in Crowborough, where he found a kindred spirit. Nellie Groves was fourteen years his senior and lived to be 101. They enjoyed listening to classical music and drinking an evening sherry together for several years. Lucy thought this was hysterical and commented that she never considered my father a "toy boy." Dad was immensely proud of his centenarian friend and died shortly after she did.

These days, I'm semi-retired and enjoy traveling with Dale. We've expanded our horizons beyond France and Spain, although they are still close to my heart. Our travel style is similar to the early days, although I've finally learned to plan and not take stupid risks, making things run more smoothly. We're still on a budget and stay with friends and family or use Airbnb, with friendly hosts in Europe and the Caribbean.

Singing, playing the guitar, and painting still bring me joy. Creativity is life-giving, regardless of talent or lack thereof, and the desire to keep exploring and expanding is part of my essence.

I continue to walk daily, alone or with others, preferably in the countryside or near water. Walking is my meditation, a conduit to my inner being. I now understand that this internal connection is what I was seeking—and sometimes finding—while traveling all those years ago. It was easy to feel connected on the farm, with the Lavignes in France, or with my friends in Spain. Learning to maintain that sense of belonging when alone has taken a little longer.

That said, I love being around and visiting family and friends—wherever they may be. Thanks for checking out my story, and feel free to get in touch. And if you hosted me in the past, I'll gladly return the favor.

# Acknowledgments

Love and thanks to Dale for his unwavering support and to Jonathan Gullery for his expertise, creativity, and seemingly endless patience in making this book a reality. Also, to Paul and Pauline Stratton, Debby Stubbs, Lucy Fairfax, Val Rose, Susie Douglas, Lionel Binnie, Chris Perkins, Antoinette Alitto, Alan Rylands, Robert Shirinov, Delah Brucelli, Debby Gullery, and Catherine Wald.

# About the Author

Pippa's childhood was spent wandering the English countryside and riding horses on nearby Ashdown Forest close to her home in Crowborough, Sussex.

Fascinated by Europe from a young age, she studied French and Spanish and spent several years traveling during the 1970s. On relocating to London, she worked at the Spanish Embassy and dabbled in freelance journalism before moving to the United States. Pippa now lives in New York's Hudson Valley with her husband, Dale, close to their three young adult children. She enjoys traveling, playing the guitar, and walking beside the Hudson River.

You can contact Pippa at typicalpip@gmail.com